Twin Flames and the Love Story Within

A Journey of Soul Awakenings, Healing, and Miracles

Emily Jennings

In memory of my twin flame who made this story possible along with many other miracles

Contents

Foreword

To write this book, I had to experience the most mind-blowing, amazing, and tragic events of my life - all within a short period of time. After the death of my twin flame, I knew this book had to be written.

I'd been writing blog posts about twin flames ever since I'd met mine. Countless people reached out to me in response to these posts about meeting their own twin flames. When I wrote about my twin flame's passing, more people contacted me who had experienced the same thing. "At least I'm not crazy," I thought. I started coaching others in their twin flame journeys and trying to make sense of it all, even in my own grief and pain.

There are so many of us in pain. I hoped that in writing a book about this journey, it would heal and help a lot of people.

Whether your twin flame is with you physically or not, you must remember that this life is ultimately your own journey. Important relationships of our lives, such as that of a twin flame, are mainly there to awaken you to new heights of awareness. A twin flame especially appears in your life to jolt you into a spiritual awakening.

If you step back and look at life as a path your soul set out on, then it seems more obvious why the events in your life have occurred, including the event when you met your twin flame. This is the main point I hope you get from this book. We can take lessons from every major event in our lives.

It's important to remember who you really are. Or, I should say, *what* you really are. Twin flames come in to remind you that you're so much more than a physical body. You're a soul playing a role in a big movie wherein you're usually unaware of the nature of what you're doing and why you came here. They help you remember.

There are no textbooks about twin flames. It is hard to locate any studies done about them. I have heard many stories about individuals on their twin flame journeys, but my findings are not scientific, and I have not quoted any of the people I've spoken with. If you've met your twin flame, then this book will make sense to you. If you haven't, this book is not intended to convince you that twin flames are real.

I don't think anything in this world could make you believe in twin flames until you've met yours. That is the nature of twin flames. They come into our lives to bring us faith in things that are not necessarily scientifically proven. Some knowledge comes from the heart instead of the senses.

Read this book with the goal of taking your confusing experiences in this strange lifetime and learning some spiritual lessons from them. I will give you a quick guide for figuring out whether you've met your twin flame, and then the rest of this book will be an analysis in chronological order of the twin flame journey. Perhaps your journey will not include all the stages explained here, but I hope that they can offer a guide as you step through the most amazing adventure of a lifetime.

Introduction: What Is a Twin Flame?

Twin flames are said to be souls that share the same mission. I see them as partners on a journey, sitting on the astral plane side by side watching the universe unfold.

They are destined to meet in human form. I believe that *they* plan it that way. As humans, the road can be bumpy and even turbulent. But twin flames are not turbulent in their soul form. They're trying to achieve something together. It may seem like a wild and crazy journey from our perspective as living creatures but looking at it from a higher plane of existence, it's all playing out exactly the way it's meant to be. They push each other toward something greater.

Twin flames are also mirrors of each other. When I looked into my twin flame's eyes, I saw myself. When I spoke with him

I heard myself. He seemed to understand me at my core, and his behavior seemed to mirror mine. His insecurities were also mine and watching him was sometimes uncomfortable because it was like watching myself on video.

There is no one else in the world (who I have met so far) that can make me feel this comfortable and uncomfortable at the same time. I can't express how surprising it feels. No one can warn you about it ahead of time or fully prepare you, because there's no comparison for the feeling of meeting a twin flame. It just creeps up on you when you first meet them.

In my experience, someone who says they don't believe in twin flames just hasn't met theirs. Why? Because before I met mine, I was absolutely certain that twin flames are totally made up. I was being fairly arrogant about it, even. I thought I knew everything about reality and there were no surprises left. *How wrong I was!*

Just days before I met my twin flame, I was telling a spiritual friend that soul mates are real and we have many, but twin flames aren't real. I was drafting up a blog post about it, too. I was going to lecture the world on how ridiculous the idea of twin flames sounds. Literally just then, my twin flame entered my life. *You just can't make stuff like this up.* He took my life by storm and turned it upside down. It was quite a lesson in not allowing myself to think I know everything about reality.

Part of the experience of meeting your twin flame is the universe telling you that you know nothing. Reality can change at any time. Miracles are possible.

You'll know if you've met your twin flame. It's like a dump truck running into you, spiritually. It's like a metaphorical ton of bricks falling on your head. There's no way to ignore it and no way to look away. You will have absolute certainty about the reality of it, and it will defy all sense and rationality. You will never be able to logically explain it to anyone else. It's a huge test of self-trust.

Meeting your twin flame and the journey that follows is also a journey of trust and inner wisdom.

Months before meeting mine, a good friend of mine had been talking all about her twin flame. She said they'd met and then separated under extremely unusual and strange circumstances. I had remembered that she said this person made her feel like she was in a black hole and she didn't know what was up or down for days, or even weeks. It was so intense that she couldn't focus on any other parts of her life. It was like a vortex had sucked her in and rearranged her whole existence.

So, when I met mine, I started to feel like I'd been sucked into a black hole, and in remembered her words to me. Not surprisingly, upon our first meeting, he said he was listening to a podcast on black holes. *There are no coincidences.* I said, "That's funny because talking with you these past couple of days makes me feel like I'm in a black hole. In a good way."

It was a confusing ride, but wonderful beyond belief. It was a spiritual awakening. In the chapters that follow, I will describe every part of this awakening journey in as much detail as I can.

You'll find in some online literature and media about this topic that many people will describe twin flames as two people sharing the same soul. I don't know if twin flames share the same soul or if they're split souls. I don't have any experiences to support that claim. I don't know if all the information you can find about twin flames is true or not. Why? Because twin flames make you question *reality*. So, *I say*, anything is possible. But I don't personally define twin flames as literal twins of the same soul. They seem to be individuals to me, with a very deep and strong connection that they cannot ignore after they meet.

I am not even against the idea that there could be more than one "twin flame" for you in this world. One seems like enough, especially when you're muddling through the painful journey, but since anything is possible, there could always be another journey like this waiting for you with another person.

As I will talk about later, doubts are normal in the twin flame journey. You might have them every day. The whole thing makes you doubt everything you knew about life, so part of that is doubting whether twin flames are real. It wouldn't be *right* if you didn't.

Sometimes I think the universe just wanted me to believe in twin flames in order to get me to the final goal of soul evolution. The whole plot was designed to get me to wake up further. Maybe all that matters is the result and the mode of transportation there can take many forms.

Romance is not the point of this journey. It isn't happiness, either. Unfortunately, it isn't even supposed to help the universe make sense to you. These things might be aspects of the twin flame journey (they were for me at certain stages!) but ultimately, the goal is self-love and soul growth. It's about *you*, not them. The introduction of a twin flame into your life path wildly changes your perspectives and pushes you to be a better version of who you are. Your existence can never be the same.

Many aspects of this journey manifest in similar ways for all twin flames, so it can be helpful for you to hear about my own experiences. In this book, I'll offer you some insights - some which will be useful whether you've met your twin or not - and some of my stories may offer healing for you.

My story is unique to me, as all twin flame journeys are personal. They fit the relationship and soul journeys of the specific souls involved. This story is only one that can be added to countless twin flame stories from all around the world. I hope that it helps people understand the true nature of reality and allows you to stop and self-reflect.

Please read this with an open mind. And fasten your seatbelt. Twin flame journeys are never a smooth ride.

How to Know If You've Met Your Twin Flame: A Quick Guide

More and more people are meeting their twin flames—or they *think* they are. I want to start with the basics and describe what it's like to meet your twin flame. Especially if you've just met someone who is completely re-arranging your world spiritually, there are certain signposts that can tell you if it's a twin flame awakening that you're experiencing or something else.

Twin flames share a soul mission. They mirror each other. They wake each other up. It's not about romance necessarily

It's not about happy endings. They find attraction toward each other for many reasons. It's a magical and painful experience.

There are relationships that are toxic. The universe has put them in your life path for you to learn a lesson and rise above them. Toxic situations are usually karmic in nature.

Twin flame relationships shouldn't feel toxic – they will just *make no sense*. Your twin flame may act "disrespectfully" toward you, but this will only be a manifestation of your insecurities and their own, which you share. Since this person *is you*, the behavior they display is just a mirror of what's going on *within* you.

Let's examine some of the clues that tell you that you're on a twin flame journey.

You Feel Intensity and Some Obsession

In the beginning, you will feel an intense attraction toward this person, and you won't consciously understand why. It will quite frankly blow your mind just to meet them. And you won't be able to stop thinking about them. The fact that they're also telling you that they can't stop thinking of you won't help! The attraction will almost be too much for you to embody. The world will seem to melt away and you'll feel like you're sucked into a space-time vacuum with them.

People will say you're obsessed and try to convince you that this isn't healthy. Especially when you enter the painful separation stage and you miss them terribly, your friends will try to convince you that you're being unreasonable about the whole thing. But this is normal stuff—people who have never met their twin flame will just never understand. They can't possibly know what you're going through.

Someone has just opened your heart and turned your reality on its head, so how can you hope to fully explain this to anyone who's never experienced it? Don't even try. You feel drawn to them, and you know you can't just let go of this obsession. It's not like feelings you've ever felt in the past.

Trust your heart. Go with your intuition. You're being called to gain a level of trust in divine timing and miracles that you've never had before.

They *Are* You

It's going to sound insane unless you've met your twin flame, but this person *is* you. Somehow, they are so familiar that it feels like you're talking to yourself when you're with them. It's a wild experience. And you will never be able to logically express it to anyone else.

All of us are part of each other because we are all essentially souls that are part of one big collective. But your twin flame is seemingly even *closer* to you than most souls. The connection that you feel there is staggering. You don't need to understand how it's possible in order to *feel* it.

You might feel like you're looking into a mirror reflection sometimes when you see them, although this makes no sense because they probably don't look much like you. But somehow, this face is so familiar.

Often, I would think in his voice. It doesn't make sense, but when my internal narrative of thoughts was going, it would be in his voice, not mine. But it *felt* like mine.

Their smell is familiar. Their energy is familiar. Their gestures and mannerisms are like yours. And You just feel at home with them. Why? Because you're basically the same person.

Pain. Extreme Pain.

Your twin flame will mirror your insecurities - your darkest parts of yourself. This is uncomfortable even for the strongest of us.

Being forced to reckon with your own fears is painful. Trauma will come up from the past. Realizations about all the baggage you've been carrying will knock you off your feet like a hurricane of awakenings. Any past wounds, however old, will be front and center suddenly. Whatever you're carrying in your karmic energy field will probably reveal itself in a shock.

If you try to run away from your twin flame or get angry when things get uncomfortable, it just makes things worse for you. Some people try to "cut cords" with their twins, but I don't recommend trying this. It's much better to face the pain. The pain is coming for a reason.

Twin flames might be "in love" but they also mentally derail each other. It's hard. Being human is hard. You know you're in a twin flame relationship if it's both wonderful and painful. The whole experience will drive you nuts.

They Bring Miracles With Them

When you meet your twin flame, reality will begin to shift. This is the whole point of the journey. You awaken to a whole new world and it's just wild. But sometimes it feels like a rug is being pulled out from underneath you. Strange occurrences begin.

You might begin to see and experience things that appear to go against the laws of nature. It will not be unusual to start questioning those laws. If you're someone who needs evidence for things you believe in, then this experience could be jarring. Repeated numbers, strange animal behavior, coincidences that seem too hard to believe, and any number of miracles will begin. You might even find yourself developing psychic powers.

The real miracle, of course, is that the universe has brought two people together who are simply meant to be.

Past Life Familiarity

The two souls have known each other for many, many lives. They've always been together, in the physical realm and outside it, too. They plan lifetimes together so that they can meet and achieve something spiritually great. So, it's no shocker that when you meet each other, no matter how uncanny the circumstances, you will have a deep feeling of familiarity.

You might start thinking, "Wow, I feel like I know you so well even though I just met you today." On the astral plane, you are old friends. You go way back.

In human form, many things are not clear about where we came from and how we got here. However, a twin flame will remind us that we are more than our physical forms. There's more to life than meets the eye. For at least *one* of the twins, it will be undeniable that there is some deeper connection occurring than can be achieved in one meeting or even one lifetime. Feelings of "there's more going on here than meets the eye" will be strong.

No Happy Endings Guaranteed

From my conversations with many people who have known their twin flames, I can tell you that twin flames have a whirlwind journey full of ups and downs. It's all about getting to union and unconditional love, despite all the challenges. Happy endings usually don't help anyone wake up to reality. So, the twin flames don't necessarily have fairytale endings where the two lovers get to spend their whole lives together. The twin flame stories I've gathered from people I know prove this to me.

Instead, it's often rather like a Shakespearean tragedy. There are twists and turns. People will say "this sounds like a movie!" when you tell them about it. There are a ton of lessons in the journey that can be valuable even beyond yourself.

The universe is watching this movie. It's hoping the two flames will find a way to be together - but being human is just so blindingly difficult. Life is so hard and so short. It's never guaranteed that the two flames will have that happy, peaceful ending. Sorry.

Release expectations of how life is supposed to go. This is a big lesson.

They Awaken You to Reality

The last thing I want to say about twin flame relationships is that you know you're in one if they awaken you to a **higher level of consciousness**. This is the uniting feature of any twin flame journey.

Your awareness of who you really are as a soul will come front and center to your attention. You won't be able to look away from this person who is mirroring your very existence. It will be undeniable that something strange and special is going on here, and very hard to resist the fact that it's highly spiritual.

Your twin flame changes everything. You'll never be the same again. Carry on. You are on the right path.

It's Not About Romance or Happiness

The concept of a twin flame seems exciting to everyone. Why? Well, because it inspires us all to imagine that there's someone out there who really *gets you*. Someone who shares a very deep connection with you that makes you feel like there's order in the universe. This person reminds you that there's oneness. Miracles can happen at any moment.

Obviously, you'd want to be romantically involved with such a person. Nothing sounds more exhilarating. However, I'm convinced that the point of this twin flame journey isn't romance. It's the elevation of souls.

Your twin flame may spark a great love affair in your life, but that's not the *ultimate* goal. I'm talking about the story you're living – your *life* – as just one thread in a great tapestry of the universe. It's all part of a greater design. Your twin flame exists to wake you up.

If you are lucky enough to meet your twin flame in this lifetime, they will arrive in a whirlwind of spiritual awakenings. You will know it when it happens to you. It won't be something you need to research or ask anyone about. The strangest things may begin to occur, like the remembrance of dreams you had about them before you knew they existed, or the occurrence of unlikely coincidences. It's not just romance that you'll be focused on. You'll be elated at the changed occurring within you.

A series of events will unfold which will make it seem like there's really a higher order to the symphony of life. You'll be forced to understand the great meaning in all things. The miracle of meeting such a person who restores hope in your heart that love can be real will be surrounded by the realization that all of life can also be full of purpose. Destiny becomes very real to you when you've met your twin flame. You'll fall in love with *all things*. It's wild how reality seems to shift.

They may make you feel extremely romantic and loved, but more than this, they will light the flame in your heart that awakens the ability to love unconditionally. The pure love that has always resided in you will have its chance to express itself. You'll surprise yourself at its depths.

This is the *true* miracle.

When you know how much love you're able to experience — in both giving and receiving — you are finally harmonized with the rest of love in existence. The hope for a better world is kindled. You are able to love and nothing can stop you. All the love of the universe is already within you.

It is incredibly romantic to experience twin flame love. However, the *awakenings* that result in this romance are the main event. I'm convinced that twin flames are the universe's vehicle to raising the collective consciousness to new levels. The love affair between these two people is beyond the normal realms of human relationships.

The ability to love someone who mirrors and expresses your deepest insecurities is truly magnificent because it gives you a chance to *love yourself.* Loving yourself is incredible as it unlocks the ability to truly love others.

Twin flame romances feel like they're out of a fairy tale. They're living, breathing romance novels. They're inspirations for stories like those of Shakespeare. Such an epic romance can only lead you to understand that miracles are possible. You suddenly feel an affinity for the rest of humanity because you see that all we're yearning for is that kind of connection all our lives. You've just gotten lucky enough to experience it for yourself!

Twin flames typically endure a period of separation which can last between weeks and years. It's unbearable, especially for the twin that is aware of the miracles occurring and wants to be with their other half. Facing such excruciating pain is good for us.

Only in our moments of total confusion and suffering do we have a chance to transcend the pain completely. The ability to find a way through this world even when things don't seem to make any sense is within us all. As we evolve as souls, we seek out reasons to keep believing in miracles even during the darkest night. To find the light within ourselves, we must experience shadows.

Our twin flames give us the greatest gift of all: total insanity that can pave the way toward total understanding.

The Dream

Almost a year before my twin flame entered my life, I had a dream about him. This is a common experience in the twin flame journey. The divine plan of it all cannot be as magical unless it's announced ahead of time - *so that you know it's meant to be.*

Not all twin flames remember having a dream about this person before meeting. Sometimes they just have a feeling something big is about to happen. For those with awakened psychic abilities, the dream will be more prevalent in their journey because they are more able to remember where they've been travelling while their body sleeps. Here, I'll explain my own experiences with the twin flame dream.

The term "love at first sight" gains new meaning in the twin flame journey. When you see your twin in a dream, it's unforgettable. For me, it was a dream where I met this person who exudes pure and unconditional love. The feeling overwhelmed my entire being and I awoke with a lingering feeling of total adoration that stays with me even now when I think of it. It was unconditional love. I'd never experienced that before. It felt so real.

His physical features were also clear enough to carry on in my memory so that I could recognize him in waking life.

The dream or vision you may have about your twin flame is important for your recognition later. Your soul already knew this other soul and their current human form. When you meet them, you are called to the awareness of that on a conscious and waking level. Is that not *incredible*?

This dream is a spiritual milestone. Your higher self and your Earthly self are communicating and getting ready for a great leveling-up. Premonitions are happening deeply.

Throughout the twin flame journey, dreams play a big role. I will be explaining this further in later chapters. They are always significant. This person knows you on the astral plane, so when spiritual shifts occur, why *wouldn't* you start dreaming of them?

A Milestone of Awakening

It is obvious from my talks with many people who know their twin flames that one of the twins is usually "awake" and the other is not, but close to it. What does this mean? Well, it means that when you start to undergo a major spiritual awakening which brings you into awareness of the oneness of the universe, your consciousness is elevated. Not only is it amazing to awaken spiritually, but it seems to put you in a prime position to meet your twin flame. In other words, if you work on your connection with spirituality, you may find yourself meeting your twin.

Perhaps your awakening is a spiritual beacon for your twin to find you in the physical plane. They have always been with you on another plane, but maybe the two souls wait until one makes strides on their spiritual journey before they can begin their path toward union. Maybe the universe waits for the perfect set of circumstances in order to introduce (or re-introduce) the twins so that the impact of the meeting will have its full effect.

Personally, I prefer to think that the point of twin flame awareness was predestined and planned before both souls incarnated. It's a signpost. We live in a beautiful storyline and it tells us that there is a divine plan. Either way, the awakening to a new level of reality is often concurrent with the dream which tells you that blessings and more awakenings are headed your way.

Some twin flames meet in childhood and then reconnect many years later. This is also usually around the time one or both of the twins is awakening to a higher level of being – shedding negative cycles in their lives and stepping into their power as individuals. They may strangely start to dream about each other even if they haven't communicated in a while. This can also be a sign of things to come.

The great love story that was dormant deep in your soul starts to unfold when the twin flame dream occurs. You may not be ready for the spiritual jolt of meeting your twin flame until you have awakened somewhat more. So much healing and shadow work is required in this journey, and if your soul isn't ready to take that on, it can make the road very bumpy.

Alignment

After the dream occurs, there's no way to tell how long the union will take. The point isn't to tell you that union with your twin flame is imminent, it's to tell you that something is changing. That's what I think, anyway. Consciousness is elevating. The path is clearing for you and you're in alignment with what you're meant to be doing. You attract your twin flame when you make choices to live a lifestyle that aligns with your soul purpose.

It may take some more healing and self-discovery to get to the reunion even after the dreams you're having about your twin flame. You can't force it on the physical plane. You must just trust that the universe is orchestrating this union. Stay open minded and make sure that the blessings coming to you have a clear channel for their delivery.

Most people don't realize they're on a twin flame journey until after meeting their twin flame. The dream is significant to them, but they don't understand the significance until the miracle of the first meeting. (I mean the first meeting in *this* lifetime, of course.) Sometimes, meaning becomes clear only in retrospect.

Many More Dreams to Come

The first dream was just one of many. After meeting, I saw my twin regularly in dreams. Many great spiritual messages were conveyed to me through the dream state. Often, they were hard to decipher, but the fact that he was strongly with me in my consciousness was all I really needed in order to survive this wild journey.

Let's be clear: your dreams take you to a higher level of consciousness than waking life does. You are aware of so much more there. You're able to transcend space and time to speak with other souls. You can visit situations without the constraints of physical form, so you can learn so much that isn't obvious on the Earth plane where we are experiencing separation constantly. You're *boundless*. So, don't write off your dreams. If you remember them, you need to take heed of what they mean.

Reunion: A Miracle

Meeting your twin flame for the first time in this lifetime is an awakening beyond your wildest imaginings. It's attraction on the highest level and it's also *spiritual*. Parts of you come to the forefront of your consciousness that you didn't know were there. You experience an intensity of love (sometimes coupled with fear) that you thought could only exist in fairy tales and Shakespeare plays. Life becomes wonderful and bizarre at once, and you start to wonder how you could have ever lived such a mundane life before this meeting. All other connections you've ever had with other human beings will seem so mundane.

When I met my twin flame, I felt like I hadn't ever actually been alive till that moment. All of me was awakened at once. He also told me that I excite every fiber of his being. I was embarking on an incredibly intense journey. It seemed that we needed each other badly. All of my world was in his eyes, and nothing else seemed to matter in those early moments.

Neither of us seemed to be able to fully comprehend what was happening, although I was a spiritual person and had some inklings. It was beyond my wildest imaginings. No experience in my life could have prepared me for this.

This is the fun part of the twin flame journey. Meeting someone who mirrors you and is somehow deeply connected to your soul is transformational. And it's like coming home. This is your cosmic best friend, so it feels *right*.

The universe will bring you together - *somehow*. It will be amazing and funny. It won't be anything you can predict. Often, twin flames meet in places far away from their hometowns or in situations that you'd never expect to find that kind of connection. It doesn't matter if you're born on two different continents. In fact, the universe seems to use this situation as proof of a divine plan, because what's more miraculous than these two people originating far from each other and coming together?

For some couples, the two souls incarnate in the same place, meet as kids, and then drift apart to faraway places, only to somehow be called back together again years later. Some part of their hearts just yearn for one another.

If two people in completely different places thousands of miles apart can appear together in the same room and recognize that they are meant to be together, this is a miracle. You'll *feel* it. It'll knock you off your feet.

Intensity

My first meeting with my twin was like being blasted in the face by a spiritual fire hose. Most twin flames start this way. You'll be going about your business as usual, thinking that you know what life is about, and then this spiritual tsunami will wash over you and you won't know what is real anymore. *At least, if you're doing it right.*

You may feel the intensity so strongly that you won't have the bandwidth to stop and figure out what is going on right away. The attraction to this person will pull you in. The two flames can't get enough of each other. Why? Because they have an understanding at a deep soul level that this is an incredibly significant event. They've endured part of a lifetime apart before they could be reunited.

The magnetism they feel between each other is part of the relief of finally encountering this person who had been physically separated from them since the previous incarnation. The strange feelings from a thousand lifetimes come rushing back to them and it almost feels like they want to catch up to make up for the lost time. Something about each other is just *irresistible*.

It will feel like an obsession. Other people won't understand it. You'll seem like you've lost your mind to those around you who haven't met their twin flames. They'll try to tell you there's no such thing as twin flames and you should stop and think about what's going on because this doesn't seem healthy to them. But for the awakened twin, it will be unmistakable and undeniable. Trusting what the heart tells you is important.

My twin flame and I expressed to each other that it felt like we'd been together before, and the feeling was very clear to me. He said it was like a reunification and that we'd seemed to have waited for so long. I told him that speaking with him was like picking up the conversation again after a short time ago, although we'd never met in this lifetime before. We both told each other how much we loved talking to one another. Our first conversation was like a dance, a perfect exchange of ebb and flow, and he said to me "Oh god I love talking to you." Countless times, one of us would say something and the other would say "it's like you're speaking my own words out of your mouth." We started noticing similarities between our lives right away. We'd *just* met. There is no other way to categorize this than a miracle.

It moved fast. It made no sense. The conversations we had from the very beginning were nothing like those I'd ever had with anyone else. Super intense, I felt right away like I could express anything I wanted to this person. It was so incredibly familiar, and it seemed to shock us both. We both explained to one another that we couldn't stop thinking about each other and we were enthralled just knowing each other. It was almost scary because we didn't know where it was taking us.

For me, it was enough just to speak to each other over text message, using our physical forms to communicate our love for each other on this plane of existence through a phone.

Physical incarnation is hard. It's horrible at times. It's confusing and painful. Sometimes it provides hope and light. For the twins who are united, the road is no longer lonely and a surge of intense love like nothing they've ever known starts to take over. The one soul that most relates and connects with a twin flame's energy is finally physically in front of them, and this is an insanely exciting event.

The two flames share a mission in life. They deeply understand each other. They feel like they are the same person in many ways. Life doesn't have to be solitary anymore and there is immense hope - the love that can be experienced between them feels like it may even save humanity. It's so strong that *anything feels possible.*

I told my twin flame after a few days of meeting him that miracles are happening and anything can manifest if we just ask for it. I felt like I was being blessed by the universe, and I wanted him to feel it, too. Great wonders were on the horizon for us. It was dizzying how fast we were going and how hopeful everything felt.

When we met, we both said to each other that it was like we were being pulled into another world. Reality was changing. We couldn't focus on anything but each other. Any way that I could describe the wild feeling of intensity, he mirrored back at me in his equally descriptive words.

I believe that we were *speaking* each other's souls because we had known each other for eons, for lifetime after lifetime and the lines of separation between those lifetimes were blurred. Our souls were inseparable.

It is a once in a lifetime event to meet someone who can completely share an experience with you and then express it to you in exactly the same way you express it yourself. I felt that we understood life in the same way. There are no words that can express this kind of feeling.

Intense and deep was this strange and incredible meeting. Normal life was just in our way. It felt like we needed a week together to just be shut off from the outside world so we could stare into each other's eyes. We talked of escaping the world together. I wanted normal, mundane physical reality to step aside so that we could sweep each other away to our own world for a while.

This is a big life event. However, it's often more apparent to the twin who is spiritually awakened. The extent of the miracle that is occurring in the reunification is only consciously apparent to one, and not the other. If the other twin is still living in the matrix, they likely will only know these truths at a soul level and not as much in their waking minds. It may even scare them how powerful the energy of the first meeting is. They may feel the initial wave of intensity that raises the consciousness, but then logic might start to set in. On the surface, they will resist the miracle and try to understand it as just another normal human relationship. They may run in the other direction.

For anyone not fully awakened to their spiritual identities, the reunification will be intense and wonderful at first, but it can turn into something that somehow *hurts*. Some people think that they must resist true love. Nothing can be *that* good, they'll think, and all of their insecurities will be triggered at once, causing them to flee.

We shouldn't blame them too much. Most people in this world are afraid of being consumed by something greater than themselves. Many people also feel unworthy of true love. They prefer to preserve separation of their souls and turn away from the oneness of the universe and the unity that the twin flame relationship proves can be possible – choosing, instead, to stay in fear of the unknown.

They are called 'flames' and I like to think that's for a good reason. A flame can be all-consuming, and it ends up transforming what it touches. It can burn. There is nothing peaceful about the twin flame union at this stage of intensity, but it certainly demands your attention and leaves you believing in true love.

Recognition and Familiarity

Intensity is just one aspect of the twin flame experience. Eventually, it can calm down. However, the feeling of extreme familiarity never does.

My twin flame died after we'd only been physically together in this life for a few months. I didn't know him very long in this particular incarnation, and yet he was the one person I feel I know better than anyone else on this planet. Conversations between us just flowed - always. We understood each other's thoughts and worries. We deeply cared about each other and forgave each other for any behavior.

I had unconditional love for this person, meaning that it didn't matter what he ever did in life - I would always support him and love him. That's because I felt that I knew exactly *who he was*. I understood what made him tick and his motivations were so familiar to me, that I felt they could have been mine. I felt that I knew his soul.

(Could this familiarity happen again with another person? I'll speak about this more in a later chapter, but the short answer is that I think anything is possible. So, *yes*, it can happen more than once.)

Although we had taken different life paths, we shared similar thought processes and we approached situations in almost the same way. We both felt drawn to experiencing new and unusual things, understanding the cosmos, asking lots of questions, and helping our fellow man. I would have done *anything* for him.

There were shared interests, big and small. I have never met anyone as excited about electronica music from the 1980s as I was. There was never such a person who enjoyed dancing and singing loudly in the car as much as I did. We enjoyed being silly and relaxing on the sofa with no plans for the day. We just enjoyed each other being near.

Looking into his eyes, I saw my soul. He commented many times on the magnetism of my eyes. Our eyes revealed the truth of what was really going on. The behavior on the surface between us reflected a total harmony of mutual understanding. It was like a dance. We wove in and out of mutual respect, support, and care.

Beyond the surface, our energies seemed to complement each other perfectly. Being in the same room as him brought me a feeling of total comfort and relief that everything was going to be okay. He knew *who I was*. Our souls knew each other very well.

The familiarity was so strong that we often commented on it. We expressed to each other the ease with which we could interact, and there was no fear involved in our relationship. There were strange things going on in the background, but fear of the intense connection wasn't one of them.

After the initial period of intense attraction, all I wanted to do was sit beside him. Nothing made me happier than to be beside the one person who totally understood me. My greatest desire was to sit in his presence and help him become the best human he could possibly be.

If I could support him in his life's mission and he could support me, it felt like we would be unstoppable. Joining forces in this lifetime - *finally* - was a miracle.

We have soul families that incarnate with us many times. There are people in your life who you'll run into and feel an immediate familiarity with because you've been friends in many forms before this one. The twin flame, however, surpasses this because not only have you been incarnated together countless times, but you share so much in common.

I often wondered if I *was* him. The more I meditated on it, he surer I was that the edges between us were blurred. Twin flames may not literally share a soul, but on other planes of existence, they aren't really separate. The familiarity you feel when you meet your twin flame reflects the fact that you may actually be *the same person*. And this is reality's way of letting you taste the oneness of all souls and all things in existence. Maybe we are all the same as everyone, after all.

Many times, it would hit me that if I was a man, that's what I would act and look like. I would wear the clothes he liked (we practically wore the same clothes as it was) and I would wear my hair like that. It was sometimes strangely uncomfortable looking at old photos and videos of him performing because it felt like I was watching myself. It was not just as if I was looking at someone I loved, but looking at *myself* and seeing my own insecurities manifest. I could see my own mannerisms and presence in this world just by *seeing him*. Any weakness I felt that I had seemed to be clearly shown in his own life.

We are not just bodies made of genetics and biology. As souls manifesting ourselves into the physical world, our consciousness actually shapes what we look like. The same physical traits will manifest across lifetimes between incarnations. The soul determines what we really look like in life.

Have you ever noticed that if you really work on yourself and change your life for the better, either by becoming healthier or pursuing a lifestyle that is more fulfilling, your face and body *actually change*? It's not that stress is taking less of a toll on you. Your soul is actually able to connect more deeply with your modus apparatus as a human being in this world - your body. It is more aligned with your higher self. So, it's no surprise that your twin flame will look very familiar if your two souls have been together many lifetimes. You've both incarnated in similar bodies many times.

The twin flame experience of looking at *yourself* is surely there to help elevate your soul and draw attention to your issues and problems. It's always a journey in self-healing.

Later in this book, I explain how *separation is an illusion.* I'll say here that twin flames teach us that we are not separate. We are not individual souls alone in the world, victims of the whims of fate. We have love surrounding us. We are connected - *all of us.*

Twin flames just awaken us to the fact that souls can be intertwined and deeply bonded with each other beyond the weird things taking place in our current lifetimes. But this is only a lesson in the greater oneness of the whole universe. The fact that two such people on Earth can exist, meet in the uncanniest of circumstances, and fall in love in a way that elevates their souls just shows that the universe is full of love and there are no accidents.

Everything happens for a reason.

Life Commonalities

You and your twin flame will share interests and a deep understanding of life, but you'll also strangely share similar life events. This is another indication from the universe – sometimes with a sense of humor – that this is no coincidence because it's just too fantastic.

You're both individuals on your soul journeys, but somehow life has found you to be so incredibly similar in your experiences.

My twin flame and I made big life-changing decisions in the same years as each other. There were multiple life events in our timelines that coincided, and they were major. It was impossible for me to ignore these coincidences. In addition, we were both highly social creatures and we had the same sense of humor. We had the same color eyes. We both hated pickles on our burgers. Big and small, the commonalities between us just kept mounting as we got to know each other.

Even stranger, we had close people in our lives with the *same names*. That just blew my mind. I find this to be one of the best expressions of the universe's sense of humor. It felt like it was a plant for us to find so we could recognize that this was no accident at all.

I believe that twin flames share common life stories because they have been living in parallel to each other their whole lives. Having planned the whole thing before incarnating on this planet, our lives manifest in ways that reflect our soul plans.

It also has a lot to do with similar inclinations. If you both pine for the same things, why wouldn't you find yourselves making similar decisions?

These coincidences are expressly there to help you wake up to what's really going on. Eventually, you have to understand that there are some synchronicities that are too great to merely be coincidences.

Synchronicities and Signs

Just in case you still don't believe in twin flames and you want to try to ignore all the miracles happening to you, the universe will orchestrate situations to present you with that you cannot turn away from. You may see repeated numbers, animals, and have feelings that just can't be an accident. You'll have synchronistic thoughts with your twin flame, and experience feelings like anxiety at the same time. You'll start to be able to read each other's minds. The wildest things will start to happen. You may not want to believe it's really happening. This is how you start to awaken.

For me, there were 11's. A ridiculous number of 11's everywhere. Sometimes there were 0's too. The 1's side by side signify two people coming together and a 0 signifies unity – at least, that's how I interpreted it at the time. The two souls were finding oneness yet again. Reunification was happening.

The number 11 is also a sign of soul evolution. It marks your journey to enlightenment. You're awakening. This is the number that should truly fill you with excitement that you're aligned with the universe and its great story.

Of course, all numbers are significant, and repeated numbers in general are a signpost that you're on the right path.

The more time passed, the more repeated numbers I saw. It wasn't always 11, but the repetition was uncanny. They were everywhere - on car license plates, highway signs, bank accounts, phone numbers, the clock, and even things like my follower count on Instagram and the labels on skin products. The more you come into alignment with your true path, the more numbers you'll see. As you get closer to the life you're supposed to be living and the soul-shattering events you're supposed to be enduring, they'll increase in frequency as confirmations that you're doing all the right things.

One day I mentioned to my twin flame in a text message that I'd been seeing 11's everywhere and asked whether the number 11 meant anything to him. He said it was funny because he felt a deep connection with the number 11, and immediately as he was saying so, he looked up and saw an 11 on a television. It felt like the universe was screaming at us, "This is it! The time is now!"

Another crazy thing that began happening was that I'd wake up just seconds before a text message would come from him in the middle of the night. He also commented on how strange it was that my messages came to him in such a timely manner, just when he was thinking of me or about to write to me. It was like our spirits were in sync when we were mentally communicating. We could physically be a million miles away from each other, but we would energetically be communicating.

Animals came to cheer me on through this journey. Praying mantises, tree frogs, bald eagles, and snakes appeared many times, to name a few. These animals don't really have to do with *love*, as you might have noticed. Although love is the ultimate form of expression in the universe, the twin flame journey is more about the evolution and healing of your own existence. These animals signify *transformation*. That is the step before coming into love.

Later, many times I saw animals as couples, and I knew reunion was near - especially when I saw two swans. These animals are loyal and share a deep life connection. They always appeared just when I needed reassurance of the reality of the twin flame journey.

The wildest thing by far that I experienced during this time was a feeling of warm energy that would wash over me when I was thinking of him or talking to him. It was like my heart was opening up in new ways and transforming me at a molecular level. It was both beautiful and painful at the same time. Thing were shifting in my subtle energy body that I couldn't keep up with. And of course, when I mentioned this strange warm energy, he said he was experiencing it, too, and it was like nothing either of us had ever known.

Later, I learned that this warm energy wave is sometimes called a *high heart chakra opening*. Things within my heart energy were being unlocked that had never come to the surface in this lifetime. This was important as I progressed in my journey, because later I knew I had to focus on removing the uncomfortable part of it. There was fear in my heart mixed with the love, and the fear was blocking it from flowing freely.

When these things happen, and they happen to both of you, it's just another reminder that you're connected. Space and time aren't barriers between you. The energy you share transcends physical reality. There are no coincidences in the universe.

Realizing That You're Twin Flames

You may not realize that you are twin flames until after you've met this person. I didn't even really know what twin flames were when this started happening to me. I had the strange inner knowing that I needed to google this term "twin flame" and find out more. I've heard of others who heard about it from a friend or happened to see an article about it on the internet at just the right time. There are no accidents.

After the initial meeting and recognition that some crazy and deep things were going on here, I started studying twin flames. All of the initial stages that people talk about seemed to be happening to me – the dream, recognition, and the meeting. It was obvious that this pattern had begun. I couldn't believe it at the time. It was wild and wonderful.

In this early stage of twin flame union, as I began to understand what it all meant, I saw that I was headed for the next stage: separation. If we were twin flames, this was unavoidable. I tried to tell myself that we were too perfect, and that we wouldn't need to be in separation. How wrong I was! Separation is an important part of your soul evolution, and it can't be skipped. Nothing good comes about from an easy journey.

Separation Begins: New Awakenings

In the twin flame journey, the most common stage you'll hear about is separation. Why? Because it is challenging, and people are most likely to talk about it and write about it. In this journey, you'll have the most questions during your separation stage. That's why the largest portion of this book is dedicated to it. *Twin flame separation is painful as hell.*

Sometime after the initial meeting (in this lifetime) of the two flames, and it varies between them, there will be a period when they aren't physically together. Usually, it's because one of them wants to withdraw or 'run'. The whole experience is really freaky to them. Some people don't feel ready for such intense love or they aren't able to let go of the traumatic baggage they carry within them which blocks them from true love. They are terrified of the experience and the intensity.

For the awakened twin, the journey is highly spiritual and an exciting introduction to a higher level of consciousness. Although they may also be a little scared of what's happening, they understand that this is a once in a lifetime chance for happiness. They see that this other person has brought them closer to God.

For the other, less aware twin, it's scary because they are so used to mundane reality. They're in the matrix. They're addicted.

Many twin flames meet in their youth and they're separated for years before they come together again. My journey was not like this at all, and it was somehow accelerated. We met, separated, reunited, and then more events happened all within the span of a few short months that felt like an eternity.

Your twin flame journey is very personal and won't be exactly like anyone else's. There's no way to guess how long you'll be separated. (Time isn't real anyway, right? Or so you'll find yourself asking...) This is a time to self-reflect and notice all the miracles happening in your daily life.

A lot of the separation won't seem to make any sense. Maybe you'll stop communicating suddenly without any explanation - *ghosted*. This is what happened to me, for instance. Perhaps one of the twins will tell the other that the relationship is too painful although they love the other twin very much. Perhaps there will be anger and frustration over something that no normal person would ever quarrel about.

Your friends may tell you to forget this person. In their mundane version of reality, they see this as just another disappointing interaction between two people, and they will encourage you to walk away. They may even say this is "toxic" for you. But they haven't seen miracles. Only you know what's *really* going on. You should trust your intuition.

For whatever reason you can't be together and for however long it lasts, know that it's meant to be. It's part of the journey. The extreme pain is necessary for your path to your highest self. The healing you must do is essential. It isn't supposed to be easy!

The Runner and the Chaser

In classic twin flame lore - which mainly consists of anecdotes on the internet and terms coined by word of mouth - the twin that is awakened is usually called *the chaser* because they see what's really going on and they are trying to make it work between them. *The runner* is the twin that is freaked out by the intensity and the realization that they have an eternal soul, and they want to get as far away from this uncomfortable situation as possible. They want to preserve their status quo in life, no matter how aware they are that they are deeply unhappy.

The runner may not be entirely ready for the journey ahead. They are married to the three-dimensional physical reality that most human beings attach themselves to. They may have some interests in the occult, the mystical, and metaphysical things, but they won't usually have delved too far into it at the beginning of the twin flame journey. They need time.

The chaser is the twin that is awakened and who understands the heavy significance of what has begun to happen and wants to continue and amplify this spiritual experience of love. They see beyond the physical, mundane reality that we all experience, and understand that their two souls must be united.

It's my belief that the more awakened one of the twin flames has become, the more likely it is that they will come back together. The closer the less awakened twin is to accepting this incredible experience of spiritual ascension, the shorter the period of separation. When both people can recognize that this is an experience beyond what they normally expect in reality, things start happening to bring them together.

Separation only happens for healing and recalibrating. If they're both almost there in the first place, then the separation won't be as necessary. The two souls work as a team, and the more healed one of them has become, the more healed they are as a unit. So, this is why you should try to heal yourself spiritually and emotionally all the time.

The chaser feels the heartbreak of being in separation with the one person on Earth who can fully understand them and who makes them feel less alone in the world. The runner feels the fear of losing themselves into a love that is all-consuming. Separation is hard for them both, but between them, there is a difference in the level of consciousness about the pain. Only when they both heal can they come back together.

As the chaser, I learned very quickly that my goal is to find deep self-love and to heal my trauma. I had to release a lot of karmic baggage that was still weighing on me from my past. My lack of self-trust was the first thing that came to the forefront. I needed to develop my intuition - but more than that, to learn to *trust* it.

Nothing can make sense in the twin flame journey. When you try to make sense of it all, you find yourself swimming through an abyss of madness. My twin flame stopped communicating with me for seemingly no reason at all, and very abruptly. For most people, this is called "ghosting" but for me, I had to trust myself that this was part of the twin flame insanity, and that this person would eventually come back into my life. Other relationships that were mundane and less meaningful would be written off as a situation of "ghosting" if the person stopped talking to me. But this was different. It was *always* different. The problem is: there was no way to explain this to anyone logically.

However, I *did* tell people I had met my twin flame and that he was not speaking with me. People tried to encourage me to forget him and move on, but I told them I knew he would be back someday - I just didn't know *when*. I told them that there was no other person I had ever met who I could imagine being with. And so, I would wait.

Some part of me knew it would be about two months, however, and that's exactly how long it took. Your higher self - your *soul* - knows what's up. It will always know what's coming. You just have to learn to listen to it and trust it.

My only task during this time of separation was to *heal, heal, heal*. I had to commit myself to it with my whole being and work with my spirit guides to achieve it. I got pretty crazy with it, too. It started like a spiritual hurricane.

Shadow Work

The next day after I had stopped hearing from my twin flame, the healing journey started with a bang. This may not happen for you, but it's important that you focus your attention on the healing work you must do for yourself. Not just at *this* time, but always.

Shadow work is the act of intentionally healing things that have been carried for years within your energy field. Traumas and baggage that you've endured shape your fears and anxieties and can really block you from living a good life if you never face them. You'll carry these problems with you all your life and into the next life, too, unless you stop to look directly at them, allowing them to surface and heal. It can be insanely painful or scary. But it's essential. The longer you postpone this process, the harder things will be for you.

My story of shadow work was pretty weird. My 'shadow' actually attacked me and forced me to pay attention. What follows is an account of my shadow work that I was thrown into right at the beginning of my twin flame separation period.

I was camping in the mountains next to a magical lake, on a beautiful weekend when the campground was full of visitors. My daughter and I slept in a two-person canvas tent. I sat with the campfire for a good while after the sun went down, imagining that the fire was burning away my karmic baggage and attachments. I was *asking* for healing and for the ability to elevate myself to something better.

After having trouble falling asleep because of some inner turmoil, which certainly explains the rest of this story, I awoke — or so I thought — to find a dark, shadowy man sitting at the picnic table outside the tent. Clearly, my perceptions had acquired supernatural powers since I could sense this man there without sitting up in my sleeping bag or opening the tent windows. I *just knew* he was there. It was vivid and more real than any feeling that you or I usually have in waking life.

I tried to call 911 from my sleeping bag — an attempt to contact someone for help through dreamland's cell service. (I certainly hope I wasn't really on my phone trying to dial it!) The operator on the other end — from the dream realm — informed me that my health insurance wasn't the kind that allowed anyone to come out and assist me at this time. Absolutely ridiculous, but I believe it was a message from the universe that I had to do this healing on my own.

I addressed the shadowy figure who was still seated at the picnic table, facing me. I think I asked him what he wanted or told him to get lost. He got up and came at me, attacking the tent! It was terrifying. So, I yelled for help.

I screamed "Help me!" three times, and it felt really hard to scream that out loud. The sound couldn't come out of my throat at first. That's because I wasn't dreaming — I was using my *real, waking voice.*

This is when I fully jolted my awareness back into the physical world. My heart was racing, and adrenaline was shooting through my entire body. It was after midnight. I just held onto my chest in the tent, trying to prevent my heart from beating out of it.

I heard people talking from nearby campsites. I hoped they hadn't heard me. Lights came and went in the darkness - some from cars and some from flashlights. The forest held other sounds of acorns dropping and animals moving, so it was hard to tell if a human was walking nearby or another creature. (There are far more creatures in the woods than our five senses know about.)

I found later that some other campers had actually called the rangers because they heard me calling for help. It was super embarrassing.

I knew I needed to heal. It was time for something to change. I reflected a long time on what happened to me that night.

I woke up at the campsite in the morning light and realized that this was **my shadow** coming out to haunt me. My shadow had visited me in the night and presented me with a very real struggle, and it's with me *all the time*. There's no escape. I needed to find my way out of the karmic cycles that ensnare me. My shadow was giving me prime opportunities to do so by confronting me so dramatically.

I wanted to end this once and for all and give it an ultimatum: *I'm not scared anymore, shadow! Don't mess with me.*

This was my time to overcome blockages. To stop being afraid. To not let my ego take over my life. I walked around the campsite talking to my invisible shadow like a crazy person. "If you try to bother me again, you're going to be surprised, I can promise you that."

I haven't seen it since.

Healing takes many forms. You may think that all healing rests on the surface of life where you can observe it with your eyes, but there is so much more about us that we need to pay attention to. You have the power to heal yourself and you don't need to rely on someone else to do it for you. All you really need is self-awareness to get started.

See yourself for what you really are and identify your wounds.

More Synchronicities and More Signs

As the twin flame journey progresses, through separation and union, the synchronicities remain strong. That's because no matter how painful it all feels, you're actually on the exact right path. You just can't see it from where you are now. The signs are giving you the guidance you may seek.

For maybe the first time in your life, you're right where you need to be and you're ascending just as the universe hoped you would. Alignment is happening.

The repeated numbers may become so extreme that you start to wonder if you're losing your mind. Are you seeing a ridiculous number of license plates with 333 on them? Are you always looking at the clock on when it's on the 11, 22, 33, 44, and 55 minutes of each hour? Are there wacky signs you see on the highway that just randomly say 111? If this is happening to you, it's both mind blowing and normal at the same time.

At one point, I just gave up thinking deeply about it because they were so constant that I started wondering if numbers were ever real in the first place.

The strangest things continued to occur. I felt called one day to open a book of short stories that was on my shelf to a random page. I started reading the story on that page, and it contained characters that sounded like me and my twin flame, and one of the characters was even named Emily. Imagine that! The storyline sounded like a twin flame story, too, and the ending was uncanny. The story described *us*. Things were getting weird. It actually described a similar ending in the story to what had actually happened between us.

In a dating app I had installed, I got repeated and consecutive "matches" from men with his same name. This was just wild. You can't explain *that* away! I knew it was a sign from my guides or whatever force was above me that I needed to believe, trust, have faith, and he would eventually return to me.

Animals were also paramount in this synchronistic journey during twin flame separation. For instance, I had a frog land on my lap while I was meditating the day before I met my twin. A frog! On a third-floor balcony, no less. I went hiking and saw a pair of swans in the wild. I don't live anywhere that swans are normal to see. And they're common where he is from, ironically. Swans are also a classic sign of twin flame reunion. I knew separation wouldn't go on forever.

I also continued to have vivid and intuitive dreams.

It's all there to remind us that there is no separation. Everything is the same. Numbers are the same. Time isn't real, there's only the present moment. People aren't separate. Maybe I'm not real. Animals are really reflections of *us*. Things aren't random. Everything happens for a reason. The world is full of meaning.

The seemingly random universe starts to make sense when this stuff has been happening for a while and you simply can't look away from the "coincidences" anymore. So, the twin flame journey is always accompanied by the communication between the universe and you so that you know you're not alone.

Weird Psychic Powers

I didn't know what *clairalience* was before all of this began to happen, but when I started smelling his scent every now and then, I wondered what that could mean.

It was a "phantom" scent. I might be standing in my home, where he'd never visited, and I'd get a whiff of how he smelled. It's something you can't just reproduce in your mind easily, and when I'd smell it, the memory of him would come back in full force. It certainly wasn't "really" there and yet I distinctly smelled it.

I learned that clairalience is the psychic power to receive messages via the sense of smell. I thought it was one of the strangest things that could be happening to me.

I smelled *him*. I smelled things that weren't there. I smelled cleaning liquid, cigarette smoke, perfume, hotel shampoo, you name it. It was not easy trying to figure out what significance it had - but later, of course, it all made *perfect* sense.

Developing intuitive powers is a common part of the twin flame journey. If you're feeling the call to investigate the mystical side of life, don't ignore it. The changes you're enduring will be on all fronts, and this is your chance to get closer to the spiritual realm.

Dreams were part of my newfound ability to speak with spirits and foretell events. My dreams were in sync with my twin, showing me events happening to him spiritually and messages from him. They also foretold the next day's events many times. Often, they gave me instructions from the spirit world. Sometimes, they were just dreams of us together enjoying the presence of one another even when we weren't together physically. After he died, I dreamt I went to the spirit world to find him. The list of my heightened powers in dreams goes on. Twin flames are connected strongly through dreams.

Dreams aren't just your subconscious working out problems, I *know* that for sure now. Dreams are your boundless self as it manifests in a realm of higher consciousness, and you absolutely can speak with other souls there. You can find answers there. It's a place to work out your problems. You can do pretty much anything you *want* there!

Twin flames unlock each other's psychic powers. The messages presented in dreams are real communications from the souls on the other side - your soul, theirs, and other souls, too - and so much meaning can be derived from these messages. Spiritual journeys unfold in your dreams. It's no wonder that dreams become totally wacky when you meet your twin flame. Your spiritual awakening has been jump started and so much needs to be worked out urgently. Dreamland is a great place to work out past trauma and analyze what's really going on.

In addition to clairalience and dreams, my psychic connection with my twin flame manifested sometimes as a deep knowing. I sensed certain days when he was stressed and anxious. I could just tell that the anxiety I was feeling wasn't coming from me. I had to learn to trust myself in my intuition about what was happening with him, although there was no physical-world communication going on at all. At one point, I was sure that he was dealing with a family crisis, which later I confirmed. I could never have explained why I thought that at the time, but there it was.

Your psychic and intuitive feelings can guide you on your twin flame journey. Instead of looking outside yourself, desperate in the search for answers, stay calm and look within. Everything you need to know is already there.

Extreme Pain and Losing Your Mind

Twin flame separation is extremely painful, as you'll already know if you're experiencing it right now. It will make you feel like you're losing your mind. Transformations begin in separation because the pain forces you to reach higher levels of your own existence. To stay one step ahead of the all-consuming insanity, you adapt. You grow.

Either by strange events in the universe that you don't understand or through their freewill, you are being prevented from beautiful union with someone you perceive as perfect for you. All you do is pine for this person (particularly if you're the "chaser" in the dynamic I mentioned earlier in this chapter) and yet you seem to have no control over their return to your life. You wonder whether the universe is just cruel. Nothing seems to make sense.

The degree to which things make no sense forces you to re-evaluate reality. Your understanding of the very building blocks of life are challenged.

You've had a taste of true love. Life-changing love. And yet, you're unable to have that in your life every day, unable to reproduce it because of physical separation. It seems like the universe would never allow two true lovers to remain separate in such a way.

The "runner" in the twin flame dynamic will be experiencing pain too, but in the form of extreme fear. The thought of the other twin will make them want to run for the hills because facing them is only going to force them to look within. They are terrified of looking at themselves and understanding a higher level of consciousness. They don't feel that they deserve that kind of real love. They want to stay comfortable in the slightly uncomfortable world they've known till now, although the magnetism of the other twin pulls on them inexplicably. They must heal from this fear.

While waiting to be reunited, you'll be experiencing crazy synchronicities and getting signs from the divine realm. The way the universe begins to behave is incredible. "Coincidences" and unbelievable events will occur in your life. It will fly in the face of the laws of physical reality that you thought you knew. Suddenly, it will seem like there is great meaning in life and the universe. And yet, your twin flame, who feels like the only person you want to share it all with, will be nowhere to be found. This is the epitome of pain.

Some twins make it clear that they want nothing to do with the other one. They could break up with a ton of drama involved. Others fade away for years with no quarrel, only to reappear again when existing family situations and marriages prevent such a union. Mine did neither of these things. He simply stopped communicating with me for a couple of months with no explanation. I started to wonder if he ever really existed in the first place. It made no sense.

I even lost my mind to the point that I wondered if *I existed*. I'll admit, it was kind of fun having an existential dilemma!

Through all that time when I was losing my mind and crying in pain because I thought that there was no one else on the planet who could really understand me, I got stronger. Somehow, although it was so intensely painful, I became better at being human. I became resilient by understanding the universe as a symphony of consciousness that's working flawlessly to move toward love. By seeing myself as a quantum blob of energy that can heal itself, anything became possible.

Twin flame separation will all but kill you. This is how it's meant to be.

Surrender and Patience

Eventually, some acceptance sets in. Your twin flame is separated from you and there's not much you can do about it. You must understand that divine forces brought you together, so they are keeping you apart now for some kind of very good reason. The reason just doesn't seem clear to you in the moment.

You've come a long way after meeting your twin flame and realizing that there's meaning in every part of existence. You've ascended. The spiritual awakenings continue. You've survived intense pain. So, with blind trust, you begin to surrender.

Trust in the universe. Trust in yourself. This is not just a journey involving one other individual, it is a spiritual journey with the rest of creation. The universe has opened the door for you to realize who you truly are. Your own inner wisdom and intuition tell you what's really going on and your task is simply to accept this and wait. Now all you can do is enjoy the ride. You can do your best to live life. Try to love your own existence.

Maybe you can try to reach higher states of existence along the way. Maybe there are higher miracles and there is higher love waiting for you that isn't as confusing and painful as the twin flame journey. Open yourself to any possibility, you never know what will come along!

In the next chapter, I will approach the conclusion of the twin flame separation period. Here, we have arrived at its climax. It is incredibly painful as long as you hang onto any fears or anger about your twin flame. Now is the time to just relax and let the universe arrange the miracles.

Learning to trust divine timing is very difficult for most people. It is your greatest lesson in the midst of twin flame separation. When you can give into the idea that you don't have control over everything in your life and you don't *need* to things get a little more interesting. The divine forces that surround you will recognize that you're at least attempting to have trust in them, and they will make note of this. Your growth as a soul never goes unnoticed by the rest of creation. Good things can't help but begin to happen.

Separation Concludes: Elevation of Consciousness

During my own period of twin flame separation, the first part seemed to be about awakening to strange new abilities and truths. Facing my own inner wounds was a definite theme. This is what I explained in the previous chapter. But for the latter part of the separation period, reality really seemed to deconstruct for me and the boundaries between "possible" and "impossible" became blurred. Nothing can surprise me since I went through that phase. My blind faith that this person would return to my life was coupled with a strengthened connection to the divine.

Mind you, this journey is 99% about spiritual awakening, self-love, and consciousness and a very small percentage about romance. It's about you, essentially. You're experiencing yourself through the mirroring of the self in another human.

Self-love is a huge part of this journey because it involves surrender. Surrender is the act of letting go and *trusting*. You can only do so when you thoroughly trust yourself and love yourself. Likewise, you can only trust and love yourself when you've allowed yourself to deeply love the universe and every soul in it. We are all one, and the more you realize this, the less separation will matter.

Twin flames just introduce us to the beginnings of what's possible in life on Earth. They open the door. They let you understand that you are connected not just to one other human, but you have the potential to be connected to all other humans. Anyone you meet could be the next "big someone" in your life who teaches you who you really are.

When you understand that you aren't separated from the rest of reality and you're supported, then you stop fearing what *could be*.

Separation Is an Illusion

You and your twin flame have never been apart. Don't ever forget this. On the astral plane, you've been sitting side by side all this time. (And maybe others who you haven't even met yet have been there all along, too.)

We come to these Earthly incarnations to experience separation from the source, to forget that we are souls, and to get back toward oneness as if we're bumping around in a dark cave trying to find the light. Imagine sitting in the dark feeling like you're totally alone but realizing that this person has been right beside you the entire time. That's your twin flame. (And possibly some other members of your soul group, too. I explain later in this book that you may have more than one twin flame.)

When you're physically apart from this person, it is merely an illusion. Your bodies don't matter that much - they're just vehicles in this short human journey. They're manifestations of your consciousness. But in a less physical sense, there is no separation. As time and space fade away, the separation they present are less prevalent.

You're an eternal soul and your truest nature isn't physical. So, anything you experience on Earth is part of a layer of physicality which presents life to you as if it is normal and 'real' to be separated from other souls and the great soul that is the universe. But this is not a clear representation of reality. Everything is connected in ways that this manifestation can't always reveal fully. You're a spirit that is experiencing human existence. Your twin flame is, too. You're here to find each other and overcome the barriers that separation presents.

It is no different for them to be across the globe from you or across the room. You're in two bodies, and while in these bodies, you can never really be in total union. It also makes little difference, spiritually, if one of you dies and leaves the body while the other is still living. Your spiritual forms didn't move.

The time this person has been physically in front of you matters so little. It's the impact they're having on your life just by having bumped into you that counts. There will be no other character in your life that causes such radical changes to the story by just meeting you even once.

Keep this in mind as you miss your twin flame. They're not really "gone" at all. They're still right next to you in spirit. The deep connection you have with them cannot be masked fully by separation and physical reality.

This helped me immensely as I progressed through my twin flame journey. Later, when we were once again in each other's presence, I remembered that this is merely a comfort. He was always around me in consciousness. I could learn to feel him there, and you can, too. It's a great reason to develop the intuitive abilities I described in the previous chapter.

Doubting Reality

At some point in your journey, the doubts you have about the whole situation will escalate from just wondering what the hell just happened to you toward wondering what *reality* even is. You'll start to lose your mind a little. Maybe a lot. This is the fun part of the twin flame journey.

Just remember to thank the universe and your twin flame for this wild and crazy experience, because no one else could have ever made you question reality and evolve yourself in such a way.

The further I descended into the period of twin flame separation, the less reality made sense. I began accepting that separation is an illusion, that all things are one, and that there's no boundary between me and all things. I doubted my own identity. *Who am I?* I didn't believe that I was *me* anymore. I wondered if I was real. Could I wake up tomorrow and be someone else? I pondered such questions deeply. I accepted the infinite possibilities of reality and nature.

You will feel sometimes like you *are* this person. And sometimes you might question whether you're a distinct person at all. Maybe yesterday you were someone else, and today you woke up as *you.* In this journey, anything feels possible. If you're doing it right, you start to let go of any assumptions you ever had about reality, including those about your personal identity.

I felt like I was losing my mind many times. This feeling was really coming from my journey down a road of *losing all assumptions.* Your mind as you know it operates on certain ideas of what reality is made from. When you meet your twin flame, certain assumptions immediately begin to fade away, such as those about coincidences and the randomness of events. If you go deeper and deeper, you discover that nothing is real. Life is fluid. Things appear solid but they can change at any time, and your reality is a mental one.

You might come to the conclusion that the universe is a quantum manifestation of an all-encompassing mind with great order and love in it. Your identity comes out of a realm of pure consciousness, and you may realize at least once a day that you know nothing of what you really are. Anything can be true at any moment.

This journey of self-analysis and self-realization is a strange one, but it's amazing. Sometimes, it is a dark one. All of it is necessary for your growth.

People around you may seem to be living in a totally different dimension than you as they appear to happily go about their day-to-day lives, leaving you feeling alone in wondering what the meaning of it all can possibly be. It's a lonely road to walk as you've ascended from this mundane level of consciousness. You are looking deeply at what it means to be *you*.

This is the turning point for the twin flame journey, and you're on exactly the right path. Don't resist the wild and wonderful experience of totally losing your mind over and over. It's the reason you're here. It will eventually pass - *sort of* - and you'll find yourself in a new world. Your consciousness will be elevated.

Your twin flame did what they came to do. They blew your mind and turned your world upside down.

Doubting Twin Flames

During the writing of this book and many times before, I have doubted many times whether twin flames are real. I wonder the following things often:

- Are twin flames real or have I been fooling myself?
- Did the term 'twin flame' get made up to explain something that we don't quite understand?
- Was this person my twin flame or is there still something more extraordinary coming my way?
- Could there be more people with the same level of soul connection with me?
- Are twin flames mirrors of each other, twin souls, or just people who drive each other crazy?
- Did the universe just want me to believe in twin flames as a kind of trick?

- Did I dream this person up and was it ever even real?

I had many doubts, and this just became a normal part of the journey for me. It accompanies doubting *all* of reality! If you're experiencing doubts, it's perfectly normal.

As part of losing all assumptions about reality, you have to learn to trust yourself. Your inner truth is that your twin flame is *real*. It's all real in the sense that this soul is highly special to your soul and they've started you on an incredibly spiritual journey – possibly the spiritual climax of your lifetime!

There are almost no resources in the world telling you about twin flames, and a heck of a lot of voices in the world telling you that twin flames are fake. That's part of why I've written this book. But you also need to find your inner wisdom.

Trust yourself. Give faith to your intuition. This journey is about knowing yourself and loving yourself. How can you love yourself when you give credence to information outside of you before you believe what's in your own heart? Give yourself some credit.

Twin flames are real, but their definition may vary. You may define them differently from day to day. I came to realize that what's real is that I am amid a crazy period of spiritual awakening like no other, and it was all started by this one person. I'd never met another human who could wake me up so thoroughly. I'd never met another human I felt so familiar with although we'd just met. Maybe more people who can embody these traits are yet to come into my life, and I am open to that.

What I've experienced because of him is uncanny. This is real, and no one can convince me otherwise.

Separation Anxiety and Physical Effects

During separation, if I started to doubt whether twin flames were real, I would get anxiety. If I started creating any kind of separation in my mind, I would have a real panic attack. People told me to "cut the cords" or walk away, and when I attempted this, I ended up being very sorry. The anxiety would creep up on me out of nowhere.

Imagining that I was wrong about it all and that he was just another normal human being would cause a rift, spiritually. If I told myself that the relationship was mundane and toxic, the feeling of butterflies in my stomach would start almost immediately and become debilitating. The world started spinning and I was dizzy at times. Anxiety came out of nowhere. All I could do was lie down and try to remember the truth within myself.

After this happened three and four times, I learned not to seriously doubt the reality of this twin flame experience and never to try to mentally or spiritually sever ties again.

The anxiety I felt was an energetic consequence of misaligning myself with my soul or my higher self. As we align ourselves between mind, body, and spirit, we are balanced and healthy. When we deny something hugely important about our souls, the energy that interacts with our bodies between the nonphysical and physical realms becomes out of balance. It stops being in sync. Denying something so spiritual about our fundamental nature can cause us problems on a physical level. If we know the truth from our inner source of wisdom, why should we ever doubt that?

So, my advice to you is to never deny a truth, or you will face the consequences. In your heart and soul, you know what's real. You know what's true. If you try to take a different path or attempt to believe something you know to be false, you will find yourself in a predicament. When you turn your back on your own inner wisdom, you may find that even your body reacts in strange ways.

In addition, it's not uncommon for twin flames to experience synchronistic anxiety. If one of the twins is feeling sick or panicked, the other can feel that, too.

I know some days I could feel strange stress for no good reason. I found out later that my twin flame was likely experiencing some kind of breakdown at that exact moment. Such a strong connection spans the physical, mental, and spiritual levels, further reminding you that it's all really happening, and you can't deny it.

Seeing Miracles

As you ascend and find yourself understanding a new level of reality, you may begin to witness the strangest things. They may be things that defy laws of nature or things that make no logical sense. What you've been taught or have ever known comes into question. These things also may have nothing to do with the twin flame, but they only start to happen after you've met them.

Your friends just won't believe you. If you choose to keep these things to yourself, you might start to feel like you want to isolate from the rest of your community.

I went outside one night and had a conversation with my spirit guides, as I had been doing many nights. The sky was particularly clear, and the stars were very visible - something somewhat rare for the suburbs. I saw a shooting star, and that stunned me. I hadn't seen one since I was a kid! I just stared at the sky dumbfounded.

I'd been asking for a miracle or a sign for many days, especially because I missed my twin flame but also because I just needed something good in my life. I wanted some sign and connection with the divine. And there it was.

I suddenly recalled that the night before, I had dreamt of shooting stars. It was a foretelling dream.

But it didn't stop there. As I was reeling from the shock of the shooting star, above me, right around the Pegasus constellation, I witnessed the strangest thing of my whole life until that moment. I saw what seemed to be another shooting star, but this time it was moving in squiggly lines, erratic, zooming all around the sky, and then disappearing near the horizon. I was stunned. I saw it another few times that night, and then again about a week later.

What I witnessed was not just a miracle but a sign. I never thought it was an alien spacecraft. I knew that it was a form of confirmation that I had support in the stars. My spirit guides, my guardian angels, and any other forces were creating a miracle for me to witness so I could be awakened just a little more to the fact that the universe is not as it seems to the logical mind and that there are wonders beyond our imaginations.

It restored faith in me that what seems impossible is indeed possible. There is infinite potential in every moment we are alive. Miracles can happen at any moment, changing the course of life forever.

In your twin flame awakening, you may find yourself seeing things that, like the rogue stars I saw, are unexpected and unexplainable. This is the team of divine forces giving you a message. The message is: "We can rearrange things whenever we choose, and you are fully supported." It also means you're on the right path. Things are exactly as they should be.

Spirit will not cause a miracle or a glitch in reality for just anyone. They do this for *you*. You have reached a point in your journey where you needed it, or a point where you've attracted it. This is because you're *ready*.

Understanding and Loving the Self

With the knowledge that you and this person are *somehow* one and the same, or at least very deeply connected, you can begin to heal them just by healing *yourself*. Your energies are connected in such a crucial way. If you undertake the mission of healing your past trauma and truly loving yourself, then it can only benefit your twin flame – and all others around you.

Raising your vibration and the love within you always sends waves of that energy outward to the universe. It can only do good. The difference with the twin flame is that you might *actually* get to see the healing working in synchronization.

"Self-love" takes on a new meaning on the twin flame journey. People who have never met their twin flame can only imagine self-love as *directed inward*. But as you've met someone who represents a deep part of you - someone who makes you feel like you're looking in a mirror - you are able to feel love for someone that represents the *love you feel for yourself*. The more you're able to feel boundless love for this person no matter what they do or say, the more you're able to love yourself and forgive yourself. You are one in the same.

Twin flames who are lacking in self-love will have a harder time overcoming their problems so they can be together in union. But that's the whole point of the journey. Self-love is a very important reason why you've met your twin flame. You have the heightened awareness to see that you need more of it. You can see that they're lacking in it, therefore you are lacking, as well. Now, you're getting the opportunity to practice self-love by seeing your flaws in another person and then overcoming them.

You're getting a chance to forgive yourself by seeing your mistakes manifested in another human being.

Loving yourself has everything to do with healing. When I began the healing journey, I asked for opportunities to heal every day in a prayer. I didn't ask for it to be easy. I wanted it fast. And when you ask for healing fast, *brace yourself.* It isn't a clear and linear path.

Part of loving yourself means being okay alone. When you open your heart fully, you don't need constant confirmation that you're loved or lovable. You already *know* it. That's because you already direct love toward yourself, so you know you're worthy of love. Moreover, loving yourself means you're happy alone, within the love you generate all by yourself.

We are not separate - all is one. All things in the universe are the same. You may think you're alone, but you are totally connected to the entire universe. The experience of being human makes us forget this aspect of our existence. However, you have all the love in the universe within you, and you don't need to seek it outside yourself. You can love yourself by *loving everything*. (And vice versa.)

When you believe that you can only have love when it's given by someone outside yourself, you limit yourself to love that can be given and taken away. Instead, you should try to understand that the love within you is eternal, it is constant, and you can tap into it whenever you need it. It comes from an infinite source. Being "alone" isn't scary. You're never alone because you are totally connected to the rest of creation.

Twin flames teach you that you must love yourself to truly *live*. As long as there's something in your heart that you don't want to love about yourself, you will struggle with all love you encounter. Your twin flame reveals all the things about your shadow that you struggle with.

The minute you decide that it's wonderful to be alone within your own love, then you will never struggle to feel the love. It will be endless. But getting to that point isn't easy.

I realized toward the very end of the separation period that I had a lot of fear in me. Sometimes, when I had been thinking of my twin flame, I had felt a pain in my heart that was very uncomfortable. What had started as a hot rush of energy all over my body was becoming a mixture of joy and fear that struck my soul. I knew it needed to be healed.

One day, I sat down to meditate on that pain in my heart. It was a concentration of fear preventing my love from being fully expressed. I imagined the fear being extracted from my chest area, drawing close attention to it. I had some strange fear of being loved and of being consumed by this love that left me vulnerable. I started to understand that I was running away from this pure form of love, although I felt like I was consciously running toward it. I was afraid of receiving love, though I was very comfortable with giving it. In a surprising way, *I was actually the runner* and not the chaser.

Giving love is often so much easier than letting it in. It takes a very open heart and a ton of self-love to be able to receive love in a healthy way. So much fear was surrounding me, telling me I wasn't worthy of love. Of course, if I wasn't worthy of self-love, why would I be worthy of love from *someone else*? I was afraid of opening my heart to be a channel of love in both directions, and it was holding me back. My heart was embracing that fear. So, I had to remove this dark part of me.

I asked for the healing and removal of this dark part of my heart that was afraid to be so intensely loved. As I did so, I felt it moving out of me in a stream of healing. The pain was almost too much to handle. I endured it as long as I could and then I had to stop.

After that, I felt like the gates of my heart where universal love comes through were more open than they'd ever been. I was ready.

Outward Feelings Should Be Inward

Twin flames represent the oneness with all things. They are you and you are them. When you feel some frustration toward them, I recommend immediately directing that feeling inward to find the healing.

Are they treating you badly? See how you're treating yourself badly inside you. Are they hiding secrets from you? Decide how you're denying some truths within yourself.

When my twin flame ignored me and cut off communication for a while, I looked within to see where communication within myself was stifled. Was I refusing to look at some corner of my own psyche? Was I cutting off communication with some voice within me that needed to be heard? This realization is part of the healing.

In your journey, remember to take all the ways you want your twin flame to behave and apply it to yourself *within*. Decide how you should change your inner life as a reflection of the relationship you see unfolding before you.

Who's the Runner and Who's the Chaser?

It was revelatory for me to understand something very important about "the runner" and "the chaser" dynamic in this twin flame relationship. In some cases, the two people are actually running from each other. How is this possible? Well, *the chaser*, who is usually more aware of what's going on and spiritually awake, is sometimes unable to face their own inner problems. Only when they stop and look within themselves can they heal and let go of baggage that they've been carrying.

Sometimes *both* people are feeling unworthy. Any problem manifesting for one of the twins is likely also manifesting in the other. One of them is just less able to fully recognize the soul significance of this feeling. Both people may need deep healing.

So, reflect deeply on what you're doing. Maybe all this time, you've thought that you were chasing, but in fact, you were running from love. Maybe you have a fear of it that you never fully processed. Think on that.

Union: Return to Oneness

The whole point of a twin flame journey is to find **oneness**. When your twin flame arrives in your life and you enter a period of separation, it is very painful, but you must remember that there is no point in the beginning of this journey unless there is a chance for union in the end.

Our lives are scripts and we are playing roles. The plot has to make sense otherwise there's no point in this production. The insanity can't just be insanity, right?

Every day of my separation from my twin flame, I asked the universe, "Why would you introduce me to this wonderful person and then take them away?" I knew within my own heart that there was always going to be a reunion, it was just a matter of time. The universe doesn't play around.

Now, I can't promise that a *happy ending* is guaranteed. Every twin flame journey is unique, thank goodness. So, hopefully yours will result in happiness. What is happiness, anyway? Having even met such a person is a miracle, and this should elevate us immensely. Whatever comes, if you got even one day with your twin flame, this is cause for celebration.

I want to describe what it feels like to be reunited with your twin flame after a confusing, painful, and weird separation. Please take a moment to promise yourself that when you make it to this point in the journey, you'll never take a single moment for granted.

Relief and Recognition

My twin flame seemed to take time to realize that we had a deep connection beyond what we both might ever understand in the human realm. I can't say I know everything he had been feeling in our period of separation, but I suspect that the experience of ascension was as uncomfortable for him as it was for me, and he was at least feeling anxiety.

Perhaps his feeling of anxiety was perceived as very different from mine, but I believe that this period in his life was whirlwind - just like it was for me.

When we rekindled the conversation and relit the flame after being separated for months, he told me that he was hit with the realization that he was in love with me and that it scared him. I had already healed my own fear, as I described in the previous section of this book. So, I understood his fear, because it can be both an exciting and terrifying thing to fall in love so deeply with someone that you lose yourself a little bit. It scares most people to experience "love at first sight" and a deep connection that encompasses all things after only knowing the person for a short time. And we all know that spiritual awakenings can be the most fearful thing of all – something twin flames inevitably face.

Don't expect this relationship to unfold like any other you've ever known. There's strange fear involved. The intensity can make your twin flame shut down. You also might find yourself shutting down!

It's beyond anything in the physical sense – something divine is pushing you both together, and it is sometimes too much for the roles we play on Earth to embody. People need time to realize that true love is happening to them, as inconvenient and strange as it may seem in the moment.

It's so important to give and receive love equally, just as it's important to show deep trust by giving and receiving the possessions and resources you have. Lay yourself open - all the parts of your mind, body, and spirit - to your twin flame with ultimate trust in them. Trust that this love is real, and they will not hurt you. Run away, and you'll find yourself in a predicament of self-fear.

To totally fall in love, as I learned from this experience, is to totally trust at a spiritual, emotional, and even physical level. Merging into the other person means sharing *everything* without question. I was blessed to experience *unconditional love* through the presence of this man in my life.

Trouble in Paradise

Even when my twin flame returned to my life after separation, it wasn't total peace. And this was no surprise for me. I *knew* it wouldn't be peaceful and trigger-free since I was still healing, but I *did* think it would be happier times. It turned out to be the happiest time of my life, although very short lived.

Twin flames cannot follow a clear and easy path. Even after my twin flame was around me almost all day every day, I felt the need to release a lot of trauma and emotion. I was so happy to do it, too, even though it was painful.

I cried every day, just a little. The things he said to me about his own anxieties would trigger me to look at myself. I was forced to face my own fears. *This is what twin flames do.*

If being around your twin flame is highly uncomfortable, then this just means you have a lot of releasing to do. Your energy field - your *karma* - is a lot of memory and baggage that your twin flame will rub your face in without even knowing it. You must endure. You must face it. Running away from that pain is not going to do you any favors.

This person is the greatest gift in your healing journey, and I recommend that you embrace it. But it's going to take courage.

If they make you upset, look within. If they make you feel like running away, look within. If they force you to face a situation you've been karmically facing for years or your whole life, look within. *Now* is your divine chance to do so.

See what you really are. See the part of yourself that they represent and understand why it is so uncomfortable to do so.

Understand your wounds. Accept that you have healing to do. Try to alter the way you respond to situations and make a new path for yourself.

Higher Love

Although the twin flame journey as we experience it in human form is characterized by turbulence, there are moments of peace and *absolute love*. It doesn't take long to realize that the love you experience with your twin flame is of a highly divine nature. There is nothing that can compare to this feeling.

To know this kind of love is an incredible, mind-blowing experience. It brings with it an awakening to the fact that the universe is in harmony with itself, nothing is an accident, and real love exists. Therefore, everything makes sense. There is divine order in all things. You look at your love, this person who is a miracle, and then you can't help but look at the world around you with total love.

I loved my twin flame deeply for all the ways he triggered me to look at my own flaws and inner conflicts. I thanked him and still thank him for all the ways he turned my life upside down to get me to wake up to a new level. I love myself because of him.

True love is from the soul level, and that kind of love is uncomfortable to face as human beings because we are always trying to resist confronting our true natures. But soul love is greater than any feeling that comes from the ego level.

Events and situations that other souls bring to you are a part of a divine plan. Though painful, the plan itself can be incredibly loving because it helps you ascend to a new level of awareness. It transforms our lives and our existences as souls. It's a higher form of love. It's beautiful.

In union, you and your twin flame will experience a bumpy ride until you, through very difficult inner work, let go of your karmic baggage and work through your trials as a human. Your soul must also cleanse itself of the negative and harmful cycles it has been in. It's not easy. You must learn to let go and surrender. Fear can have no place in your energy field. Stop hanging onto things!

This love is greater than ourselves. It's part of the universe's love that guides all of creation to a higher place.

The love of your twin flame will make you want to achieve your soul purpose. You may notice that you start considering new career paths or become interested in mystical things. You'll also have a deep desire to help them achieve their soul purpose, too. Both of you will share a similar or identical purpose in life, and it will be something about helping other people. *Helping other souls.*

Just by finding this love, something in you will be so awakened that life won't look the same. Life will feel miraculous. The idea of *romantic love* will take on a totally new meaning because it is no longer about the ego. It isn't about acquiring material possessions with this person - not money or social status - and it isn't about keeping from loneliness anymore. It isn't about getting affection or attention or validation. This kind of love puts you in sync with the divine love of the universe. You will start to live from the soul level instead of from the ego level.

Twin flame love helps you love yourself and derive happiness from mere existence. If you can remember that this person is always beside you in the spiritual sense, then you'll never feel desperate in fulfilling worldly desires. You'll feel happy just for being alive.

This kind of love is transcendental, and whatever happens, count yourself as extremely lucky if you even get to experience union with this person for a day in your life.

Death: Unexpected Separation

Twin flames are human. They die like all people do. Your twin flame may die before you or you may die before them. Either way, it is important to know that the spiritual journey of twin flames doesn't end with death. Very little ends with death. Love certainly does not.

After speaking with many twin flames as a spiritual guide, I have learned that when twin flames die young, it never seems to be under circumstances that make any sense at all to the other twin. It's a total shock.

What happened to me was unexpected, so I encourage you to cherish every day together with your twin flame as if it's your last. What makes it so extremely shocking and painful is that when you go through this journey and finally come together with your twin flame, you come to believe that there is so much love in the universe and everything is going to have a fairytale ending. When it doesn't, it's devastating.

My twin flame and I experienced separation through his death not long after we met. Having met the person who awakened me, filled me with hope and light, and introduced me to unconditional love, I was only given a few months with him in this lifetime.

Our time together was enough for me to understand that separation is an illusion and that there is nothing that can really keep two people apart who are spiritually connected. It was also enough to raise my consciousness to levels I'd never fathomed. In life, knowing him forced me to trust my intuition. In death, he only reinforced the intuitive abilities I was becoming familiar with.

What Is Death? Separation Is Still an Illusion

What is death? Well, I can tell you that if you experience the death of someone very close to you, divinely connected like my twin flame and I were, then it's immediately obvious that death isn't the end of that person. They continue. The body is a very small part of your whole existence, and when it's done with its journey as an instrument for your current role and current life, you leave it behind. Nothing that is essential to *you* is lost.

The first hint that this person persists may come in your dreams. If you're very spiritually conscious, you will remember your dreams more and more. The dreams that involve this person who you've "lost" will become very vivid.

On the spiritual plane, you still mingle as you sleep. Your soul goes to the astral plane when you're resting your body.

I started this book by describing a dream about him that I had almost a year before I ever met him. The dreams of him continue, and they are just as real as they ever were.

My dreams with him took me to strange scenes where we crossed paths, travelled on the same roads, or found hideaways together. Strange modes of communication were also a large theme of these dreams. Learning to communicate beyond the physical realm was an important piece of what I've been through. You, too, must trust that you have ways to transfer messages energetically.

On the night before I found out about his passing, I had a dream that I went looking for him. No one yet knew that he was gone. I dreamt of him very vividly that night. I saw him with his relatives in a very peaceful, joyous, and wondrous place. He was happy to see me and said he was doing "just fine." I found no reason to be alarmed.

The next day, I visited a psychic medium. She said that I had traveled to the spirit world. It was only a confirmation of what I already knew.

In dreams, we can experience heightened states of awareness. We can travel to the "other side" and know things that we might never know as waking humans. There's so much to understand about ourselves, and our day-to-day life just isn't enough to make this journey full and meaningful. Pay attention to your dreams; they are part of the soul growth of this life. They offer such valuable insights.

You may also feel that your twin flame is still with you all the time after they pass on. In the heaviest days of my mourning, I felt that I could hear him speaking to me. It's like he was standing in the room trying to say something.

There is no separation. Death is not the end. Just as in physical separation, you can energetically sense this person no matter where they are.

Anger, Sadness, Grief, and Spiritual Awakenings

When my twin flame died, I was mad at the universe. I felt cheated. I didn't understand how I could be so happy and have achieved union with my twin flame, only to have it all be taken away in an instant. I still feel angry at times.

This person arrived in my life accompanied by a rush of emotions in facing my shadow and left abruptly, causing an explosion of sadness. It taught me that just when I think I have things figured out, life surprises me again. Nothing is off the table.

Staying alive isn't a requirement of this twin flame experience, apparently. It's all about the awakenings that ensue. If a soul's path to awaken can be best chartered through a period of grief, then that's what's going to be planned by the universe. And there's probably nothing anyone can do about it. The script has already been written.

It's an act of love from the universe to present you with *any* situation that pushes you to get stronger and more aware. As souls, death is only a transition, not an ending.

I was so pissed off. It was like I had worked so hard to "manifest" what I sought but this event was there to teach me some horrible lesson. I had worked on myself and healed a lot. I had taken all the cues from the universe to awaken to a higher level of reality, and it was awful at times. I filled myself with love and tried my best to let it all in. I thought when I achieved union with my twin flame, I was home free! I had won the spiritual lottery! I earned my gold stars.

I was arrogant; I thought I deserved peace and happiness for a long while. I thought everything was going to be just as dreamed.

I was flung into a pit of despair in an instant. From sheer happiness to maddening grief in the blink of an eye. I went through periods of the deepest sadness I'd ever known. If the love and happiness in being with your twin flame is the highest goodness of your entire life, their passing will feel like the most painful wound.

Perhaps when you finally transcend the pain of human existence and all the grief, you can see the cosmic harmony in it all.

Life is fleeting, and for those of us who are on a path of awakening, we must come to terms with the fact that it's all about awakening further and further until we've reached enlightenment. Anything tragic that happens to us must be about this, and about our mission in helping others. We can't expect life to be sunshine and rainbows all the time. That wouldn't help us get better. We must remain uncomfortable.

So, through the sadness, I saw the ironies, messages, and lessons in everything happening to me. I can't say this process is easy. I am human, too. Some days I am so angry or so sad that I can't see clearly. But if I gave into those emotions, it would be because I am hanging onto a very narrow view of the meaning of life.

It's Like *You* Died

Twin flames are so similar that anything that happens to one of them will feel like it's happened to them both. If one of them dies, it will feel like the other did, too. It's strangely like mourning your own death. *Isn't that mind blowing?*

This person is your cosmic best friend. The person who truly understands you. When they die, you will feel like you've lost the chance for anyone in this world to understand who you are. You feel like part of you died with them. It's horrible to imagine. How could anyone else ever reach that level of connection with you? A large void is left in your heart.

A part of you dies with your twin flame. It's self-mourning. You will struggle with its loss for a long time. Maybe forever! But perhaps the goal is to surrender to the loss. Understand that everything happens for a reason. So, you must try to find the beauty in the loss of this important part of your life. There is still meaning somewhere.

And I always believe that there is still hope. There is no telling what life will bring you today. You may be limiting yourself by believing that there can never be a connection deeper than this. Keep an open mind and heart to accept what other miracles are coming your way.

Things Happen for a Reason

After my twin flame died, a psychic told me that there are no accidents. This happened to me for a reason, she said. And I didn't lose faith in the great meaning in all things even in this tragedy.

If we are twin flames, then we are eternal. Our relationship is eternal. It spans many lifetimes and incarnations. So, I started to wonder about soul contracts. Surely, if every lifetime is meant to help the soul grow and nothing is an accident, then the major things that befall us in life are pre-planned. They're part of a design. Perhaps our human minds can never comprehend the divine design behind things, but it will all make sense *later*.

If you believe that everything happens for a reason, then even the deaths occurring around you are happening *to you* for a reason. Everyone dies, but when someone dies so young and in such a shocking way, it can feel like there's no justice in this universe. It can be hard to accept that there was some purpose and design behind *that* event. I still have trouble accepting it.

Our egos get in the way of comprehending the behavior and design of the universe. The ego is the part of you that creates separation and individuality. It creates anxiety in us because it tells us that there is no oneness. Our egos fear death immensely.

However, when we see ourselves as souls, death isn't scary. It's just a transition to the next awakening. It isn't the end of anything very important. From a soul level, the perspective on death can start to *make sense*.

As an experience in your life, loss can be a lesson for you. That's really painful to hear or think about sometimes. I'm not saying it's a lesson for *everyone*, but as it happened to *you*, maybe it's telling you something.

Let go. Love has been had. Good things happened. And they come and go.

Nothing is permanent. Perhaps the universe just wants us to understand this, and release the expectations of life. It hardly *ever* goes the way we planned.

Why Go On Living?

After enduring such great pain, I couldn't help but ask myself why I'm still here. Why was he the one who died and *I'm* left behind? Why should I go on living at all? What do I have to look forward to now? These questions and the grief stem from deep and earth-shattering love.

What's the point of life after you've experienced the greatest adventure? My answer is to try to let the "here and now" be everything.

Resign yourself to the idea that life is full of ups and downs and you just had the biggest "up" anyone could have, so of course it crashed down the hardest. So, I believe that you can liberate yourself from future pain by allowing the ups and downs to come and go without getting so attached. Let the pain come, but don't suffer from it.

This is a spiritual path. It's the release of expectations. You now have a chance to flow with life and just see where it takes you. Let things go and understand that you never had control.

You may also want to think about the fact that your heart has the capacity to deeply love. Not everyone has this heart opening. Not everyone is able to see beauty in life the way twin flames can. Cherish this ability. Go on and spread more love! Give it freely as much as you can. Teach others to believe in love. Let others know it's not just in fairy tales.

You can do this by telling your story as I am now, or just by loving others wherever you can. Even when we're experiencing grief, and we don't know how long the sadness will last, at least we can still add to the overall love on the Earth plane. We can expand goodness in this world a little more. Kindness, joy, respect, and loyalty are all the good things that we can still participate in.

Every single one of us has the power to elevate the oneness of human consciousness by transcending the pain of trauma.

We're the Lucky Ones

Whether you're in separation from your twin flame or they've passed on to the spirit world, you must know that you're "lucky" for just having had this experience at all. You and I - we've experienced *miracles*. We've awakened to a new level of consciousness. This person entered our lives and shook things up completely, giving us the greatest gift of all: a level-up. Let's be grateful for this. Most people never get this chance.

To know that in this vast world, there is or was a person just perfect for you, and somehow fate brought you together - that's *magic*. This is the stuff you've been taught only happens in children's stories.

That this person could find you in this great world, like a needle in a haystack, is just incredible. There is no doubt that there are no coincidences in this human life when you've experienced something so unlikely. Billions of people on this planet, and you found *them*.

Whatever tragedy befalls you and whatever may come, please know that you are one of the blessed. You've met your twin flame. You have an extraordinary life, and an incredible story to tell.

More Miracles and Loves

When my twin flame died, I went to a psychic. I was stricken with grief, but I had to know what it all meant from someone else's lips. She looked at me, held my hands, and said gently: "This happened to you so you could know that you're able to love. And it doesn't seem possible right now, but you will love again and you will meet *another twin flame.*"

I thought that was silly – how could I have more than one twin flame? How could I go through another experience like this one?

Since then, I've started to believe it. There could be more than one twin flame. Why would I limit myself by believing otherwise?

My twin flame journey made me believe that anything is possible, and the universe is always going to shock you. So why wouldn't there be someone out there with an even greater spiritual experience to show me? And why can't we have more than one person who shows you the true love found in fairy tales?

Anything is possible. I found myself, after my grief subsided, believing in miracles again. If it can happen once, it can happen again! And it can happen bigger. How arrogant of me to think I'd experienced it all.

Don't Ever Assume You Know Everything

Once you meet your twin flame, it's tempting to think that the amazing experiences in your life have now been exhausted. At least it was for me. But if you think you have nothing left to be surprised by in life, then I can almost guarantee that you'll block whatever miracles are coming your way.

One day, I realized that I was blocking the possibility of a new incredible adventure with my rigid beliefs. Why can't we have more than one twin flame? The universe already proved that the most unimaginable events are possible. So, why can't life surprise me again?

Don't get caught up in the thought process that you know everything there is to know. Don't be spiritually arrogant; allow yourself to be open to many truths – sometimes ones that contradict each other. You don't have life figured out. Just when you think you do, it will smack you in the face with a new surprise.

Remember, you've already learned that the laws of nature are flexible. Always stay open to all possibilities. You never know what will reveal itself next. Perhaps you haven't experienced it all. Perhaps meeting a twin flame isn't the greatest and most wild thing that could happen in a human lifetime.

Your other, future human relationships might be more mind-blowing for all you know. Other events in your life could be more amazing than this human relationship stuff, too. Your relationship with the divine is always going to be more miraculous than anything.

Maybe the next greatest thing is just around the corner for you.

Anything Is Possible – Even Multiple Twin Flames

Your twin flame turns your world upside down. Your ideas about reality melt away and you experience things that make you seem crazy to your friends.

Your twin flame helps you experience universal love. They help you understand that the impossible is possible.

I think there can be more than one experience like this in a lifetime. Twin flame experiences are so crazy as it is, so why wouldn't *anything* be possible? Your twin flame teaches you that reality is never as it seems, so why not? More love lurks in the darkness waiting for you to find it.

If you've experienced Earth-shattering love once, then it's almost a guarantee that you'll experience it again – and it can only be better next time. Why? Because you've learned to *love*. Love can only get deeper and deeper.

We also must learn to love ourselves the same way we would love others. While we wait for the next miracle, it is always possible to give ourselves more love.

If there's one twin flame for you, why can't there be another? Or – possibly – something *better*? You've learned that you're able to experience and produce unconditional love. So, your heart is open. Why wouldn't you be able to find that higher love in yet another human being?

More good things can come. An open heart doesn't stay dormant. With more and more love to give, you will inevitably attract more into your life. It's practically your *duty* to give your love to others now that you've learned how.

We call them "twin flames" but I don't want to be committed to this term. I think we can imagine ways that this could mean more than just *two*. Flames can spread and multiply, and in nature, we have triplets and quadruplets, quintuplets, etc. Twin flames might have the possibilities of being triplet flames, am I right?

Is it so strange to think that we might find a soul mirrored by more than one other soul?

Miracles happen. We know this because of twin flames. They show up in our lives making the impossible possible. Why can't there be more than one miracle? Why limit ourselves?

In any case, we are all mirrors of each other in some sense. We are all one. Not just twin flames, but everyone. But some of us are healed enough to really allow love to happen in a big way. I'm talking about *true love*. Maybe triplet flames are possible because we're actually all connected to one another, some of us are just less blocked than others from the connection.

I accept that I could be wrong, but I really do believe that anything is possible. My twin flame taught me that! Reality is malleable. Shifts happen. Things aren't as they seem. Just when you think you have it all figured out, reality shocks you.

Perhaps, too, there is always hope.

When there's love in your heart to be given, the possibilities are infinite. Love is infinite. Let's hope that for all the love we're able to give, a person manifests to whom we can give it *every time*. Love isn't wasted.

Love Can Happen Again, and Better

Most people's lives contain multiple love stories. We all learn to love in many forms. Twin flame love is one of these forms. But do you have to find someone who is your mirror to your core to really experience the highest form of love? I don't think so. (At least, I hope not, so I tell myself to be open to anything.)

Have I found a higher form of divine love than a twin flame love at the time I am writing this? No. So, maybe I shouldn't be talking!

All relationships are here to teach us something about ourselves. Love will come to you again if you've lost your twin flame in physical form or if they've refused to be with you in union. As long as you seek love, it will come. Love is inevitable. Don't lose hope.

Twin flames are here to show us the deep connection possible with other human beings. They blow our minds with the awakening to reality and how all of our assumptions have been wrong. They bring us into a whole new world of realizations. They change us forever. Many of us "twin flamers" develop psychic abilities and wake up to our life purpose in helping others heal. Twin flames activate the best timeline of our lives for healing and being a fully embodied manifestation of our spirit's intentions on Earth.

None of this implies that they will be the love we spend our lives with. Perhaps they aren't meant to be there in this capacity at all. Someone who blows our reality into a new territory can't offer stability at the same time. Love can happen but this doesn't entail security and lasting comfort. They challenge us to see that life is about change and that we can't attach ourselves to things. We must learn to let go and grow.

So, love can come in other forms. A person who loves you and stays in commitment doesn't need to also be a twin flame, and they can be just as emotionally fulfilling for you, if not more so. But never forget to look for the lessons that each love in your life has to offer. Anything uncomfortable is a challenge for you to overcome some problem within yourself. If you find good love that lasts and makes you feel happy, then it is a sign that you've found that within yourself first.

Never run from or discount love with anyone who feels good to you. Love can happen in less wild and crazy ways than the twin flame can offer you. While it's an experience worth writing stories and plays about, it may not be the thing that helps you sustain a beautiful relationship for a long period of time. It may not even make you feel fulfilled and good in the way that a romantic partner should. It certainly makes you reflect on all the partners you've had, however, and when you really understand twin flames, you come to realize that you are better able to work out your karmic relationships and attract better people into your life.

It's like you can learn from your twin flame's past relationship lessons as well as your own, and then rise above all the drama to achieve a new path. You know how to love and how to be loved and you'll accept nothing less.

When you see your choices and relationships with new eyes, you can't go back. You start to want real love, and you can have it with others. You can be healed and merge with someone new who is also healed. Maybe your path is also to help heal others.

Twin flames are one of many loves you will have in your life. I don't think they're primarily in your path to give you a taste of romance. They're here to wake you up.

The Whole Point of the Twin Flame Journey

Every day, I still wonder whether twin flames are even real. I wonder if it matters whether they're an illusion. Perhaps they're accomplishing a purpose on the spiritual level either way.

I always say that "twin flame" is just a label anyway. They might have had different names over the course of human history, but there's no doubt that countless people on the planet right now believe they've met their twin flame. I want to know why this is happening.

Why do twin flames exist? How do they help the collective consciousness? Must they follow a tragic storyline like *The Great Gatsby* or *Romeo and Juliet*? I have coached many people on their twin flame journeys, and these questions always arise.

I want to review the spiritual lessons of twin flames and why this phenomenon occurs.

Soul Growth and Healing

As I explained earlier in this book, twin flames famously endure a period of separation which can last between weeks and years. It's unbearable, especially for the twin that is aware of the miracles occurring and wants to be with their other half. But guess what? Facing such excruciating pain is good for us.

Only in our moments of total confusion and suffering do we have a chance to transcend the pain completely. The ability to find a way through this world even when things don't seem to make any sense is within us all. As we evolve as souls, we seek out reasons to keep believing in miracles even during the darkest night. To find the light within ourselves, we must experience shadows.

Our twin flames give us the greatest gift of all: total insanity that can pave the way toward total understanding. They allow our consciousness to raise.

Only when the tower comes crashing down can we rebuild our realities from scratch. We must be destroyed before we can heal sometimes. We're forced to look within.

Shadow work is the act of deep inner healing by taking a candid look at the self and what baggage is being carried. This baggage, or karmic energy, stays within our spiritual selves and makes us who we are. We can let it weigh us down or we can choose to transcend it.

We all have trauma that we experience in life. That trauma, if not dealt with and released, will stay with us as a wound in the soul. Our twin flames trigger our deepest fears and force us to see ourselves. Someone who is a mirror of you can't help but do so. The healing journey begins.

The irresistible attraction you feel toward your twin flame will be met with an equally strong force of madness and rapid healing. You'll be presented with huge opportunities to look candidly and clearly at your own soul. Suddenly, you'll have the ability to see what needs to be released, surrendered, and left behind. The twin flame love that you experience is mainly about *you*. They've just given you the great opportunity to ascend in this lifetime. You've been given a chance to know who you truly are by looking into a soul mirror.

Don't get me wrong, though. Love is a big part of the twin flame journey. Romantic love on the Earth plane and divine love in the spiritual plane are important parts of the journey.

Your twin flame is someone who is with you in spirit always. They want you to reach your highest good as a soul, and likewise, your soul wants the same for them. You may be very distracted and stressed, so you're unable to see this all of the time. But try to remember that you are spiritual partners. You came here to awaken each other and complete some kind of mission.

So, when your twin flame triggers in you into a panic attack, *look at yourself.* Figure out why this is happening. Are they bringing up childhood memories that you'd rather not focus on? Are they drawing attention to a specific pattern in your life that you can't quite understand, but it keeps happening to you over and over? Are they spotlighting your feelings of unworthiness?

Unworthiness is a common struggle with all human beings, not just twin flames. When faced with such deep and unconditional love as that which a twin flame offers us, there can be crippling fear within us. We might think there isn't anything so perfect, so it can't be true, or that we have never been so lucky in life so why would we deserve to be happy now? It might really scare you that love can be so powerful and might transform your whole existence. A love that is overpowering demands surrender.

Hence, the twin flames must be separated so they can calibrate to the worthiness of each other.

There are so many chances to face fears and transcend Earthly problems. So much healing can be done if you open yourself to it. You must look deeply at yourself. Shift the focus from their apparent crazy behavior to your own.

Pursuing a Life Mission

Twin flames are two souls with the same mission. However, the mission may not always be so obvious. Earlier in this book, I described how they often share life commonalities and uncanny similarities about their interests. Beyond the surface level inclinations, the way they approach their relationships with all people around them will often feel similar. Twin flames work in the same way to be of service to the souls around them

- and so, just imagine how powerful this can be when they join forces in twin flame union!

Even without twin flame union and on your own, you can be awakened to your soul purpose by your twin flame. Their entrance into your life will give you clarity. Events of such magnitude make it hard to turn away from questions of reality and soul desires.

The universe created a miracle in bringing you to this person, and you will suddenly realize that there are no accidents at all. There is a great symphony of love and meaning that you live inside. Therefore, you may start to let go of the assumptions you'd made about your life.

The programming you have acquired about reality falls away. Your ideas about what you're supposed to be doing just seem silly now. Your divine purpose comes into view. Spiritual truths reveal themselves to you.

So, even without your twin flame in the flesh by your side, you can still pursue your life mission. You will feel compelled to do so. Your twin flame turned your world upside down and there's no going back to the "matrix" life you'd been living before.

There's a reason you're here on this Earth plane, and once you know what it is, there's no stopping you.

Oneness and Awakening

When you deeply love someone, you're channeling universal love. Loving someone this truly will suddenly allow you to love life and love everyone around you.

A series of events unfold in the twin flame journey which will make it seem like there's really a higher order to the universe. You'll be forced to try to understand the great meaning in all things. The miracle of meeting such a person who restores hope in your heart that love can be real will be surrounded by the realization that all of life can also be full of purpose. Destiny becomes very real to you when you've met your twin flame.

Meeting your twin flame allows you to see that nothing is an accident. The universe makes things happen just as they should. When you see this, you understand that *all is one*.

Hopefully, your twin flame will also wake you up to the notion that we have experienced many past lives before this one. This is just one story among many, playing out for the good of all humanity.

This awakening should put you at ease. It should allow you to see that you're here for a reason, you're fully supported and connected, and there's nothing to fear. It should get you to the understanding that stressing about daily events is pointless. All you need to focus on is alignment with the greater elements of existence.

Whatever happens with your twin flame, just by meeting them and receiving the messages they bring - *just by allowing your mind to be blown* - you have leveled up and done something greater than yourself.

Unconditional Love and Self-Love

I'm convinced that twin flames are the universe's vehicle to raising the collective consciousness to new levels.

Every feeling you have toward your twin flame is a feeling toward yourself. If you can love this person, you're in love with yourself. It's a dance of true balance and self-awareness. Loving yourself is incredible as it unlocks the ability to love others - not just your twin flame but *everyone*. Your love is endless.

Such an epic romance can only lead you to understand that miracles are possible. When you are open to the possibility of miracles, you begin to love everything. And you feel loved by the universe.

However, you must *find* that love. Sometimes it's hard to love your twin flame when they're driving you nuts.

If, on the other hand, you have been able to deeply love your twin, they will light the flame in your heart that awakens the ability to love unconditionally. The pure love that always resided in you will have its chance to express itself. You'll surprise yourself at its depths. This person could be and do *anything* and you'll forgive them. You'll simply be grateful for their presence in your life at all. This is the *true* miracle. It's the wide opening of the heart.

As I explored my own ability to love my twin flame, it shocked me. I didn't care where this person had been, what was true or false about them, or what they'd done. I just saw the soul. I felt who he *really was* beyond his human form.

Being human is hard. We are shrouded in complexities of trauma, confusion, hurt, distractions, and addictions. Our souls are underneath there somewhere. I saw straight through the muddied reality to the truth. I *really* loved him, and what was incredible is that he awakened me to the knowledge that I could truly love someone at this depth. And if I could love one person this deeply, I could do it again. He sparked the fire of my ability to see through life's complexities to the truth that we're all souls.

Loving someone else this deeply allows you to love yourself as a soul, beyond all of your own trauma.

When you know how much love you're able to experience — in both giving and receiving — you are finally harmonized with the rest of love in existence. The hope for a better world is kindled. Your twin flame lets you see that you are *able to love*. Love like this orients you with the oneness of everything.

When you have opened your heart so deeply, the love just flows out. Your heart can't help but love *everything in existence*. This includes the self.

Indeed, twin flames allow you to love yourself. There is no fear in twin flame union, so the ability to attain self-love is unlocked.

In separation from your twin flame, you're also given the chance to love yourself deeply. Through the pain, you're forced to find a solution. Being alone and knowing that there is no one in this world who can thrill you like a twin flame, you surrender to being alone - eventually. You can begin to *love* being alone.

Since your twin flame and you are one in the same on some level, then loving yourself and being with yourself should be as satisfying as being with them. When you feel lonely and desperate on your own, it means you aren't enjoying your own company, and then why would your twin flame enjoy your company? You must work on yourself and elevate your self-love to bring them back to you. Fearing yourself will only lead to them running away.

So, love yourself and you'll always be happy in your own company. It will be healing for both you and your twin flame on the spiritual level. Although they may not be near you, your own inner work will benefit you both. If you love yourself, their higher existence will reciprocate and respond. Unconditional love will spread.

Trust Yourself

During the writing of this book and many times before it, I have doubted at least once a day whether twin flames are real. It's important that you understand that this is *normal*. It's an essential part of the journey. Your intuition and inner wisdom are being developed, and the world around you is at odds with that new knowledge. The universe has just thrown something at you which seems impossible. So, it's your path now to work through the doubts and discover what is true for yourself.

When I start to doubt the reality of what I've experienced, I remember that there is no other person who has ever been able to elevate my consciousness just by being in my life. No matter what my twin flame ever did, I will always have that experience and nothing can take it away. He turned my reality upside-down. This is the most important thing that a twin flame does, and it's the uniting factor between all twin flame journeys.

And then, I remind myself of the patterns I outlined in the early chapters of this book. I remember that I dreamt of him before meeting him, that there was an intense attraction and period of separation that all twin flames experience, and that there was nothing "normal" about any part of my time with him, or thereafter. He literally altered my reality. There is no one I'll ever be more grateful toward.

When you start to doubt your sanity or doubt whether twin flames exist, just remember the journey you've been on until now. There are parts of it that can't be coincidences. It will almost feel like a script for the movie of our lives.

Perhaps "twin flame" is just a current label for something humanity has known for all of time, and the phrase gets in our way of understanding its true meaning. However, the things you've experienced can't be denied. The universe is in perfect balance just because this person exists.

The world around you will try to convince you otherwise. It will tell you to look away. Your friends will try to tell you that it doesn't make any sense. They'll tell you that this a toxic relationship. They will want you to ground yourself in mundane reality where there are no synchronicities and no miracles, and where you must guard yourself against others with fear. But your job is to know better than this and to look *within* for answers. Seek love.

The twin flame journey is about *trust*. Learn to trust yourself more. You have a direct connection with the source of creation - don't look away.

Finale: Love

What matters in this universe? Love. That's all. Anything that appears in your life will be a lesson in experiencing and spreading this divine and universal love. So, when a skeptic asks you why the universe would contain such a thing as twin flames, your response can be that twin flames help us come back to love - as many things do. But they do it in a mind blowing way!

Twin flames remind us that love is everything. It's the whole point of being alive.

The universe may flog us repeatedly with disasters, but they're all a challenge to keep loving and offering compassion. Loss causes grief and this is a manifestation of love. Loneliness is a feeling of the lack of love and a challenge to find love within. Forgiveness is the act of spreading unconditional love.

Twin flames offer us a chance to deeply love, and yet the path to union with your twin flame will be full of barriers. It's a bumpy road. We have to experience the hardships in order to fully appreciate how precious love really is. To overcome our traumas and fears in order to truly love someone without hesitation is the greatest ability any human can develop.

The universe is made of love. Twin flames are an expression of that divine love in human form. For those lucky enough to know their twin flames, we have been handed a beautiful opportunity to directly experience this divine love on a silver platter.

Whatever happens with your twin flame, this love has likely infused every area of your existence with new energy. Your world has shifted. Being touched by divine love can only wake us up to higher planes of consciousness.

Your twin flame may run from you. You may run from them. One of you may die long before the other. You may find union and live happily together. It doesn't matter to the universe what you achieved in the flesh - the divine love you are able to experience through any of these scenarios is all that really matters. It's all that really *stays* in the soul. It leaves a print on the universe.

About the Author

Emily Jennings writes, coaches, and speaks to elevate the collective consciousness through the understanding of wellness and oneness. With an inquisitive nature and a master's degree in philosophy from the University of Otago in New Zealand, she has always approached life with skepticism and wonder. This is her first published book.

Visit her website: www.wellnessoneness.com

Made in the USA
Las Vegas, NV
10 October 2023

78887244R00085